Forese

Foreseeing the Future

BASIL IVAN RAKOCZI

HARROW BOOKS
Harper & Row, Publishers
New York, Evanston, San Francisco, London

This book was originally published in England by Macdonald Unit 75 under the title *Fortune Telling: A Guide to Foreseeing the Future*. It is here reprinted by arrangement.

First HARROW edition published 1973.

STANDARD BOOK NUMBER: 06-087039-7

Contents

Prologue

THERE lives secretly in every man and woman a hunger to know the future, to penetrate the veil which conceals from mundane eyes 'that which is sure to come to pass' as the gypsy prophetess insists; to gain knowledge through some oracular method when good luck is to be anticipated or when a present bout of ill luck will change.

The most sceptical and the most fearful, as well as the most hopeful among us nourishes covertly or overtly the desire to know, to face, to be certain about, the pattern of coming events. To gain an explanation of the revolutions of the wheel of fate with the seemingly unjust, hazardous, capricious rise and fall not only of individual destiny but of that of the family, the clan or group, of nations, civilisations, continents – and indeed, of our entire world as it journeys through the vastness of the cosmos.

To learn of possible dangers ahead, to gain strength to survive day-to-day problems by the promise of better things to come, in fact to be reassured, prepared, resigned, tranquil, aspiring, and courageous on the life path are the gifts that the seer offers to men. Such, among many others, are the principle tasks to which the oracles are dedicated.

What are the things men want most to know about? What are the fundamental impulses that stimulate man's desire? They fall into a trinity – a trinity of desire. They wish for:

Food. The acquisition of riches. Power. The achievement of the dreams of ambition.

Love. Sexual fulfilment. The esteem and envy of others.

Beauty. Good health. Mental powers. Long life and immortality. Descendants.

In fact, the triumph of desire in every field.

To the humblest peasant or the crowned head, the gangster or the holy ascetic, man or woman – deny this as they may – these are the age-old wishes, hidden or apparent, that are the character patterns of humanity. The most exalted magi and the raggle-taggle gypsy fortune teller know this as well as the sophisticated clairvoyant entranced before her crystal, impressive in her elegant salon in the more expensive, if not always respectable, quarters of the great cities of the world.

What are the time-honoured oracular methods of those who claim to lift the veil of the future? What are the methods they use to describe our past, present, and future so cleverly – often for quite a substantial fee? Although we should mention that a dedicated magus of the Right Hand Path would never accept 'filthy lucre' in payment for his divinatory arts.

Apart from the oracular pronouncements given by the Pythonesses of old at such famous centres as Delphi, the prophecies of men like the renowned Nostradamus, or the detailed chartings of the astrologers (with which this book is not directly concerned), there are such methods as:

Cartomancy, the use of ordinary playing cards or the more ornate Tarots;

Chiromancy and Chirognomy, the science and art of palmistry;

Numerology, the manipulation of numbers, letters, and words;

Spiritology, various forms of 'mediumship' through the use of the planchette or ouija-board and similar methods;

Crystallomancy, trance scrying by gazing into a crystal or bowl of water;

Geomancy, by using the throw of dice, coins, matchsticks, or dominoes;

Taseology, the use of tea leaves (coffee grounds, sand or pebbles also).

Such methods of scrying are but a part of the vast corpus of the occult arts and sciences, that esoteric wisdom or magic that today is being resurrected from the grave of disrepute, rejection and neglect in which it has been all but buried in the age of materialism, of so-called common sense – when rationalism has replaced the natural knowledge of primitive peoples, the priestly arts of Egypt and Chaldea, the clear-eyed philosophy and religion of Greece, and the psychological wisdom of the East.

Alas, the rejection of this traditional wisdom was all too well-deserved for the practice of the occult arts, by both ignorant and unscrupulous men, led to their abuse. We are not advocating a return to vain superstition, to credulity, to unquestioning belief, nor to a blind fatalism; all that savours of the Left Hand Path of black magic. On the contrary, we are asking for an enquiring and an open mind. We ask that old methods should be put to the test, that modern methods of investigating supersensory powers, if such powers exist, are applied to those arts called magical, that seem to link the unseen with the seen and make a ladder between that which is above and that below. Let us investigate, let us experience, let us come to know.

Occultism is the science of things hid and the art of using the powers not commonly in evidence among the profane. These powers are latent in every man, but rarely manifest themselves save in moments of shock, distress or passion, or when deliberately cultivated by one who aspires to be a master of this true or pretended science. Because of the astonishing or 'miraculous' nature of these powers, they have in the past – and by the 'believers' of the present – been thought of as supernatural. Until recently, the rational and respectable scientist as well as the man in the street who boasts of common sense, has not accorded these powers the honour that is their due nor troubled to submit the phenomena they manifest to the methodology of scientific investigation.

Today, the space age of the 20th century, a change is in the air. Years of painstaking effort on the part of the Society for Psychical Research and the work of Dr J. B. Rhine of Duke University, North Carolina, USA, have succeeded in making this study – previously dismissed as delusion, fancy and dangerous superstition – something worthy of the attention of learned scientists, materialistic perhaps, but of the utmost integrity. It is they who have re-baptised the subject with more acceptable names, speaking not only of metaphysics, but of parapsychology, metapsychology, extra-sensory perception or ESP, and so on. After all, occultism was the father of modern science and deserves to be revered as such.

The arts of the good village witch and her coven, of the gypsy and the initiatory caravan and the trance mediumess or clairvoyant that are our concern here, are but a limited area of the far wider field covered by the whole range of 'happenings' to which the universal experiences of mystics, masters and saints testify under a greater or lesser conformity to the religious faith within which they live. The latter have woven much of their vision and knowledge into the tapestry of ortho- doxy yet penetrated, more deeply than the orthodox would dare to risk, into the causal mysteries of being and the secrets of universal nature.

We pay homage to those noble souls who died at the stake for their efforts on behalf of suffering humanity. We pay homage to the country witch and the wandering gypsy who culled healing herbs for the sick with hands skilled in bone manipulation. They too, sadly often, joined the martyrs in the flames.

Depth below depth may be probed but ever the ulti- mate must remain – the unknown. There are mysteries concerning the physical body, the psychic body, the mental and spiritual bodies that, linked together, form the totality of man. These mysteries, to a greater or lesser extent, are known by the occultist – truly a master of his art – and as yet remain unknown to the average scientist. Such knowledge is known by many names: gnostic, hermetic, cabalistic, theosophic, an- throposophic or quite simply as the 'secret doctrine',

the esoteric or perennial wisdom. Such a body of traditional wisdom, transmitted as well as ever expanding,
is concerned not just with man himself but with the
structure and operations of the whole cosmos about
which we surmise but actually know almost nothing at
all. Neither do we know – although occultism might be
the key – about origins and destinies and about the
place of man within the cosmic whole, or the real
nature and meaning of life itself.

Occultism is magic in the true sense, not just the de-
ceptive conjurations of the prestigitater. The practitioner is the adept, the magus, the seer, the master. One
branch of such magic is that of creating effects by the
aid of supposedly supernatural beings and by a mastery
over arcane forces in nature. These operations will be
considered as we plunge ever more deeply into our
subject during the course of this book. It will please
the 20th-century mind if we think of supernatural
beings in terms of speed or density of vibrations, of
electricity or light-waves, and so on. For the occultism
of the future a new terminology will have to be invented – just as for religion – if it is to have any validity
for coming generations. There must be new and acceptable ways of expressing its eternal verities. Like everything else in life there is an evil and a good, a low and a
high, a negative and a positive aspect to magic. The
magus may be a black or a white magician, on the Left
Hand Path or the Right Hand Path. To put this in
another way we can say that he has an ignoble or noble
character, or is psychopathic and neurotic, or sane and
healthy; that he works for the destruction or the better-
ment of humanity. But today we know through our
psychological studies that extremes of black and white

in separation, of neurotic or unneurotic, of unnatural or natural, of total evil and total good, are a false or exaggerated dichotomy. Rather there are graduations, a sliding scale between the one and the other so that the devil is not quite as bad as he seems to be, and an angel is not as pure as he had hoped. By their fruits ye shall know them, not by the colour of their wings!

Black magicians are evil necromancers and sorcerers who use the corpses of the dead for their conjurations and seek to exploit the shades of the departed for unworthy ends. The psychologist would say that they suffer from necrophilia: while an honourable medium or spiritualist – and there are many such although they might be said to be using a necromantic art – appear to establish good and loving relations with the dead and to transmit words of comfort between them and the living. Mention should be made here of the use of the ouija-board and similar techniques – trance-voices of the shamans, for example, which is another means of communication with those who have passed through the portals of physical death. The good augur or sorcerer guides the future of the people by interpreting the flight of birds or by casting lots and other such apparently random means, while his opposite will exploit the people to satisfy his love of power and lead them to the practice of human or animal sacrifices, to their undoing. Have there not been leaders of nations who have climbed to power over the slain bodies of their brothers and have led the people through a hysteria of cruelty to final destruction? Such men work with evil spirits, the detritus of earthly existence.

It must be clearly understood that not all witches are evil and ugly old crones, nor red- or green-haired seductive maidens who lead men to their doom. There are both male as well as female witches, and the same holds true for sorcerers who would better be called sooth-sayers or medicine men (and women). The good are proficient in the simpler methods of divination, in the art of healing and bone setting, and in weather know-ledge. They are expert in preparing charms, in match-making, and in fertility rites. Only when they turn to cursing, to the use of the evil eye, to poisoning and to working with evil spirits for evil ends, are they being seduced by the Left Hand Path. In stigmatising evil arts and in attempting to prevent them, the Church and State have been right just as a police force is right in checking crime. Even in the pagan world many of the mysteries had fallen into corruption and their use had to be discontinued, and in all societies the workers of evil have had to be constrained. But it was only when freedom of thought and the right to practise whatever religion or philosophy seemed to be good and true, when scientific enquiry and the propagation of truth grew to be anathema to Church and State, that the evil of totalitarianism and conformity overcame the rela-tively small evil done by ignorant, possibly crazy and ill-tempered, witch or wizard. With the attempted domination of the western world by the Christian hierarchy, the secret doctrine had to go underground, not daring to re-emerge without fear until the Age of Reason. It is to be hoped now that the work of the good magus will triumph and that of the bad, a great deal of which exists also, will be constrained compassionately, eventually to be transmuted just as we constrain a naughty child for its own sake or confine and treat a dangerous psychotic on behalf of the rest of society.

Those who consult a magus and the would-be student of the occult should always be on guard against the charlatan and the devotee of deliberate evil.

In this book, when we have described and explained our hedgerow methods for telling the past, present, and future, and when we have outlined the theory and practice, allowing ourselves a glimpse at the deeper initiatory and philosophical aspects of these homely arts, we will attempt to present the reader with some rationale of how these arts appear to work in so many cases and we will point out where they may fail or be dangerous.

We make no apology for dealing with subjects which many will consider superstitious mumbo-jumbo. Having travelled with gypsies, been accepted in many secret lodges and covens, the writer is unashamedly fascinated by the theory and practice of the diverse arts of divination and through a wealth of gathered experience, is convinced of their validity – although well-aware of the inexplicables involved. It need not be said that when strict secrecy has been enjoined upon the writer by gypsy master, lodge hierophant or leader of a coven, his 'yea' of assent to silence has been rigorously adhered to – 'Those who tell do not know, those who know do not tell'.

I

Cartomancy: The Art of Fortune Telling with Cards

ORIGIN AND HISTORY

THE origin of our common playing-cards and of those more elaborate cards known as the Tarot is unknown outside initiatory lodges and covens whose traditions would be questioned by the objective historian.

Were cards first used to read the past, present and future, or were they used in games of chance? This is not definitely known, but the gypsy master declares that both methods were used for, as he says, through the *vice* of gambling with cards, the *virtues* of the esoteric doctrine under glyph and symbol were preserved. 'The Wisdom of God is the foolishness of men.'

The ease with which a pasteboard pack of cards can be transported along with a few personal belongings by the nomadic gypsy favours the story that it was he who, reaching Europe in the 14th century AD if not before, carried the cards with him from his ancient birthplace in Rajputana and the Punjab through Persia and Egypt to the West – later of course to the Americas and Australia – a journey taking countless centuries. Such cards have been accredited to Hindu, Chinese, Persian, or Egyptian origin with various proofs – despite some scholars – to substantiate the story. It is said by some that the roguish gypsy first encountered the cards already in existence among the people of the lands through which he travelled and was quick to steal them and make them his own for future profit, magical and financial.

It is thought that the Tarot cards – known as the Tarot of Marseilles, or of the Bohemians, among other names – preceded our common packs. Seventy-eight cards compose a full Tarot deck of which fifty-six are suit cards. The suits are:

Cups, Grails or *Chalices*, probably corresponding to *Hearts*; in Germany *Hearts* also.

Swords or *Daggers*, probably corresponding to *Spades*; in Germany to *Leaves*.

Platters, Coins or *Pentacles*, probably corresponding to *Diamonds*; in Germany to *Bells*.

Rods, Staves or *Wands*, probably corresponding to *Clubs*; in Germany to *Acorns*.

There are four court cards to each suit: *king, queen, knight*, and *page* or *valet*. And four sets of ten cards numbered from the *ace* or *one* up to the *ten*. Added to these are the twenty-two symbolic image cards. These are called the *greater* or *major arcana* while the fifty-six inferior cards are known as the *lesser* or *minor arcana*. The greater arcana and the court cards have images that have to be viewed upright. When they fall head downwards, their divinatory meaning is reversed. Apart from the game called Tarocchi, played all over the Mediterranean countries, our simplified, probably derived, playing packs contain at most, fifty-two cards, omitting as they do the greater arcana and the four knights.

Charles Gringonneur (1393) designed cards for
Charles VI of France to divert him when he was mentally sick. Thus the cards have a therapeutic value as
well. Possibly these are the ones to be seen in the Bib-
liothèque Nationale, Paris. Could a gypsy, performing
or begging at the Court, have seen these and made a
rough copy of them? Other packs are preserved in the
Musée Carrer, Venice. Some of the earliest that survive
may be those of Baldini (*c.* 1470), attributed to the
brush of Andrea Mantegna. In the collection of the
Countess Gonzaga in Milan is the Florentine or Minch-
iate pack (*c.* 1413–1418). Among the connoisseurs of
every kind of card – of which the writer is one – the
hunt goes on, and a card here or a fragment of a pack
there is found, while many more must remain to be
discovered. Not the least interesting of such discoveries
are the cards inscribed on skin (human?) in the Musée
de l'homme, Paris. Rondels and bamboo slips as well as
cards of ivory are to be met with in the Far East, and
lend colour to the theory that the cards originated
there.

St Bernardin of Sienna (1380–1444) preached against
playing cards and gambling along with other occult
practices. Some years later, cards made their appearance in England and were forbidden under Edward IV.
They were, of course, condemned in the Cromwellian
age. However, no prohibition has ever been able to
curb their popularity. In attempting to investigate the
history of cards the objective investigator must beware
of the possibly wilder flights of fancy of both the vision-
ary and the ill-informed occultist. Albeit such intuitive knowledge as may be gleaned from these
fascinating sources may well prove to be valid in the

end. At present it is the stuff of poetry rather than of fact – born from the archetypes of the collective unconscious. It is interesting to note the effect that the symbolism of the cards has had on poets like T. S. Eliot and W. B. Yeats.

Some time before the French Revolution, when the scientific approach was not properly instituted, Conte de Gebelin in his *Monde Primitif* – himself a High Grade Mason, member of the Lodge of the Philalethians – wrote that he had encountered the Tarot, in his search for antique survivals throughout Europe, as a game of chance, a method of divination and a 'book of occult lore'.

Etteilla or Alliette the Peruqier, towards the end of the 18th century, was writing on the Tarot as of Egyptian origin, designing new and debased, if intriguing, cards with which he told the fortunes of the highest nobility while attending to their wigs. He attributed the survival of this 'book of magic' to a fraternity of the magi who guarded a temple of fire in the Levant some leagues from ancient Memphis. This book, he maintained, held the secrets of occult philosophy, astrology, alchemy, and divination. His designs were composed of symbols appropriate to these subjects. Later, Singer, who was an English research worker in this field, considered the cards to derive from the Venetian game, Trappola, said to be of Arab origination. Chatto (1848), also from Britain, tried to disabuse the occultists of their romantic claims for the cards but doubtless failed. Meanwhile the savants Duchesne and Boiteau of France were at work, the latter stressing the gypsy and Indian origins, the former remaining, it would seem, unconvinced. And continuing all through the 18th century and into the 19th, the Illuminatés of the Continent, of whom Eliphas Lévi was perhaps the most renowned, kept the whole subject of cards, magic, and gypsies veiled in the obscure writings that emerged from their lodges. Madame Lenormand, the Napoleonic revealer who was patronised by the Empress Josephine, has given her name to many charming if frivolous packs. That aristocrat, Julia Orsini, was yet another inspired devotee of divinatory cards. In more recent times the admirable and painstaking work of A. E. Waite, who had his Rosicrucian teachings portrayed in the Pre-Raphaelite style cards by Miss Pamela Colman Smith, brings the story nearly up-to-date. In France Hermetic interpretations and designs have been made by Jean Chaboseau, and there is a *de-luxe* annotated pack known as the Grand Tarot Belline. Nor must the studies of Eliphas Lévi, Papus, Stanislas de Guaita and Oswald Wirth be overlooked, and the designs made under their inspiration dating from the 19th century to the 20th. In Ireland a small but valuable study has been made by Irlande Ussher who links the greater arcana with runic letters; similarly the early Cabalists had given it the twenty-two letters of the Hebrew alphabet. Ouspensky, the Russian occultist, and the infamous Aleister Crowley made their contribution. One of the most exhaustive studies, both exoterically and esoterically, has been that of the late Gérard van Rijnberk of the Netherlands.

MODUS OPERANDI: HOW TO TELL FORTUNES WITH ORDINARY PLAYING CARDS

There are a variety of methods for laying the cards for divinatory purposes. Each seer will learn several of these before choosing and adapting that method which suits her temperament best (or his, for occasionally a man becomes proficient in this art). Generally the simpler methods are found to be the most practical and efficacious. To further clarify a reading a second method may be employed to supplement the first.

Each card has its traditional meaning which must be memorised by the seer, but each card must be interpreted in conjunction with those cards that are in close proximity to it. Finally, when all the cards have been exposed face upwards, an overall reading must be made in which any fragments or isolated revelations are woven together, making possible a summary of the entire reading. Special questions may be put to the cards after this general summing-up has been made. The wise seer is not out to astonish the client with knowledge gained through her clairvoyant powers, and therefore there is no reason why client and seer should not cooperate in learning what the cards have to say by discussion and a question and answer interchange.

THE TRADITIONAL SIGNIFICANCE OF EACH CARD

Hearts (Cups)

King. A fair, handsome and mature man. He is full of goodwill, powerful in governmental matters, he has acumen as a merchant prince, diplomatic in ecclesiastical circles. He may be of royal blood. Certainly he is aristocratic in his bearing. Open-handed, impetuous, intuitively wise, but hasty in judgments. His kind advice must be taken with a grain of salt. He may be choleric and should not get into arguments. He is the Corn King in Initiation Rites.

Queen. A beautiful, golden-haired, loving and faithful woman of voluptuous charms. She makes a faithful wife or devoted mistress. She can be a rival where other women are concerned but would not be mean or treacherous. She is the Corn Queen in Initiation Rites.

Page. A fair young man, a close friend, a confidant who may gossip; one who enjoys pranks. Sometimes perverse as he blends male and female traits. Loved by women but not always to be trusted. He is the Corn 'Dolly' in Initiation Rites.

Ace. Love, passion, warmth. The hearth and home. Domestic bliss but only under certain circumstances. A lover's tryst, even an illicit love affair.

Two. Success. Good fortune. Expectations to be fulfilled. Abundance.

Three. Unwise choices. Lack of decision. Unthought-out action. Impetuosity.

Four. Celibacy. Marriage delayed or indefinitely postponed. Anxiety.

Five. Change of environment. Difficulties of choice. Lack of decision.

Six. Bodily or character weaknesses. A too generous nature. Intrigue.

Seven. Broken promises, disappointments, betrayal, but joy through sorrow.

Eight. Gay company. Good cheer. Rejoicing. A flirtation.

Nine. Peace and success. Hopes fulfilled. The wishing card of good luck.

Ten. Unexpected good fortune, success, returning strength. News of a marriage.

Spades (Swords)

King. A tall dark man who is very ambitious. If thwarted he could be an enemy. Military achievement could lead to dictatorship. Passionate but unfaithful. Unreliable in business but having occasional spectacular success. He is the Dark God of the Witches and Lord of the Coven.

Queen. A fascinating if cruel woman. The 'Fata Morgana' type, loyal if a man is strong enough to master her. She is the Maid of the Coven.

Page. A lazy and treacherous youth who exploits others while pretending friendship. Under the right discipline he will be a good soldier but he has the nature of an assassin. He is the Devil's Disciple of the Coven.

Ace. The death card. The seer must use discretion in reading this card. It can hold the meaning of misfortune, bad news, broken relationships as well as illness or death.

Two. Disunion, separation and change. Loss of friends, breakup of a home. A journey to a far country. The card of the wanderer or refugee.

Three. The card of tears. A broken love affair or the separation of lovers through no fault of their own. Failure.

Four. Illness, loss of property, sudden poverty. Jealousy and envy destroy success.

Five. Great achievements and a happy marriage or the true partner found after a long delay. Avoid being discouraged. Patience is rewarded.

Six. Good luck after a serious setback. Careful planning brings ultimate reward but first hard work with little gain.

Seven. Tears fall. There is sorrow and suffering. Make peace with difficult relatives or neighbours. Avoid quarrels with true friends.

Eight. Read carefully any legal document before signing it. Check errors. Overcome resistances. Traitors must be unmasked. Opposition.

Nine. The card of great misfortune. War or strife can break body and mind. Perseverance will triumph if intentions are of the best.

Ten. Beware of false prophets. Trust no one until better cards are turned.

Diamonds (Platters)

King. A man of clear-cut features and steel blue eyes. Disenchantment with life has led him to become ruthless in all he undertakes. He can be a bitter rival or a jealous lover. He can be rendered understanding and affectionate only by a virtuous and tender woman. Men serve him out of fear, not love. He is the Devouring Sun in Initiation Rites.

Queen. A pretty and frivolous woman who has men at her feet. She loves gossip and scandal and arranging love affairs for her friends. Her character may be enriched only by a firm but compassionate man who curbs her excesses. She is the May Queen in village ceremonies.

Page. A pretty youth with a crafty smile. He acts as a messenger. He is trustworthy as far as men are concerned but will deceive a woman heedlessly. He acts as the God Hermes in Initiation Rites.

Ace. A letter with important news. A gift. Above all, an engagement ring.

Two. A deep or tragic love affair that will put all other matters in the shade.

Three. Possible divorce or a separation. Ruptures in business. Political unrest. Quarrelling.

Four. A broken or neglected friendship. Irritation with the family. Interference from neighbours.

Five. Splendid business relations. Honesty pays. Prosperity for the home. A life-long friendship. A happy family and joy in children.

Six. An early and romantic marriage that may end in failure. An unlucky card for those contemplating a second marriage. The caution is, wait and see.

Seven. Bad luck for the gambler. False words hurt. Gossip and criticism do harm. Keep quiet for a while.

Eight. A journey brings a new relationship spelling future happiness. A good card for the traveller or explorer.

Nine. An unexpected loan or gift makes a journey of adventure possible.

Ten. Evil influences have passed away. Good luck indeed and in the present. The client may spread his wings without fear of harm. Change old habits.

Clubs (Wands)

King. A dark man strong in body and in mind. A stalwart friend. His love for women is rather that of companionship than of passion. He makes a loyal husband and father. He is the Soothsayer of the Lodge or Coven.

Queen. A woman of an unusual kind of beauty, dark of hair and complexion. She is spontaneous in temperament, suffers sudden changes of mood, but is always loving. An excellent guardian of her friends' secrets. She is the Prophetess of the Lodge or Coven.

Page. A good-looking youth who is open-hearted and sincere. He may be given to flattery out of kindness but in reality his integrity is unquestionable. He is the Merry Man of the Coven.

Ace. Great wealth. Business success. Artistic renown. Social ambitions realised. A goodly company of friends.

Two. Be a lone wolf for a while. There is much opposition to be overcome.

Three. A long partnership resulting in marriage. Or, possible re-marriage.

Four. An accident threatens. Danger ahead. Be careful whom you trust.

Five. If care is taken and the pros and cons weighed, then a wealthy marriage will result. Be diplomatic where political associates are concerned.

Six. Excellent for business. Employers and employees work together for mutual success. The political scene begins to clear.

Seven. Beware of the opposite sex if ambitions are to be fulfilled.

Eight. Do not ask for a loan. Avoid gamblers. Friends will come to your aid.

Nine. Bad luck. This is not the moment to quarrel with friends or to break partnerships. Do nothing until a change of luck is indicated.

Ten. An inheritance that was not expected. Illness averted. A successful journey. Reunion with a long lost friend.

The attentive reader will note that there is an overall

pattern for each of the suits and certain numerological links.

Hearts tend to represent the aristocracy, ecclesiastics, politicians, and in addition pleasure and happy marriages. Their messages are warm and emotionally charged, giving joy and realised ambitions. Due to such sensitivity, sorrow and pain will be experienced to the depths.

Spades are the cards of admonition. They find expression through strength and military men are under their domination. They tell of dangers ahead and how the client can prepare himself to circumnavigate such ill-luck as they may portend.

Diamonds concern more mundane matters and are the cards of the merchant, the craftsman, and the labourer. They speak of financial matters, law suits, family stability, hard work, profit and political success.

Clubs are the cards of loyal and worthy friends. Once they were the cards of the hunter and now of the sportsman. The reverse of friendship is treason and treachery, indications of which must be looked for when Clubs are surrounded by other negative indications.

When a preponderance of any one suit is found in a lay of cards, special emphasis must be placed upon the general influence the suit will have upon the *other* cards. The kind fortune teller will always help the client to find the way to avert any bad luck indicated and to gain courage to overcome the hurdles or oppositions that may be approaching. Special care must be taken in predictions where serious illness or death play a part.

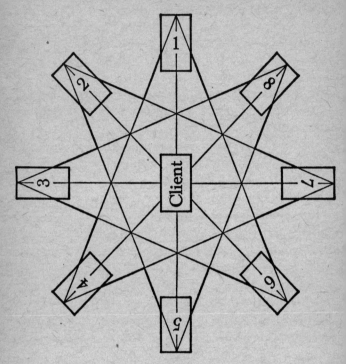

Figure 1. The Mystic Star

METHODS

In all the following methods the seer or fortune teller chooses from the pack the Court card that most resembles the client; for example, the Queen of Hearts for a fair woman.

In the Mystic Star method this card is placed face upwards in the centre of the table. The client is then asked to shuffle the pack well and to put her hopes and fears into it or, in other words, to impregnate the cards

with her astral or magnetic fluid which will be con-
veyed to them together with those vibrations engen-
dered by the emotional state in which she finds herself
at that moment. She is then asked to make three random cuts in the pack, place the cards face downwards
on the table with her left hand – the hand of the devil,
in psychological terms, of the deep unconscious that is
the motive power beneath conscious behaviour. The
seer now turns these piles of cards face upwards one
by one, reading the card exposed on the top of each
separately and then in a combination of the three so
revealed. This is what is known as giving a general
indication, and will usually show whether there is to
be a lucky laying of the cards or the reverse. Collecting
the three piles of cards together the seer now asks the
client to reshuffle them, and when this is done, the
seer takes them from the client and makes the 'Star'
as shown in Figure 1 – anti-clockwise, one card in each
point. Handing the remainder of the pack to the client,
she asks her to place two additional cards on each point
in the same order. Thus there will be three cards to
each point, all face downwards. Turning each pack of
three face upwards, again anti-clockwise, the seer reads
them in turn until she finally makes her complete
summary when all are disclosed.

With the court card of the client in the centre and
the opening three cuts as used in the Star method, the
seer now lays nine piles of three cards each as in Figure
2 while saying: 'Three above you, three below you,
three behind you, three before you, three for your
house and home, three for your hopes and fears, three
for what you don't expect, three for what you do expect
and three for what is sure to come to pass.' The remain-

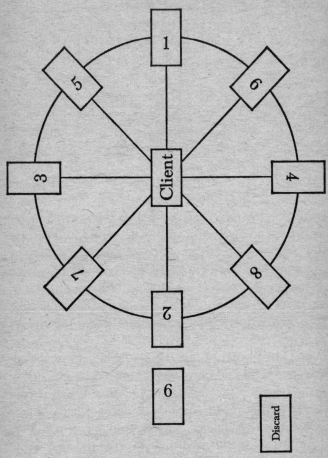

Figure 2. The Wheel of Fortune

ing cards are thrown into the discard but may be drawn upon in random sets of three if further clarifications are later required.

A client who makes too many demands at too fre-quent intervals upon the seer or who has some special

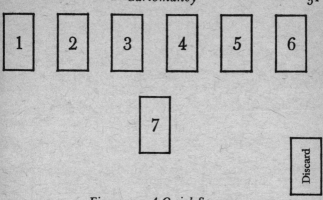

Figure 3. A Quick Sevens

question in mind may be given the 'Quick Sevens'. After the usual shuffling, the seer takes the cards and makes seven piles of three cards each face downwards and throws the remaining cards into the discard as shown in Figure 3. Turning each pile face upwards she reads the cards of each separately, then the three of each pile together and finally gives the overall interpretation.

Here the Joker, who is the fool '*Le Mat*' of the Tarots, is placed in the centre to represent the client. By 'fool' is meant the uninitiated or everyman. About this card twelve others drawn at random from any part of the pack by the client, are arranged as in Figure 4. As a coven consists of six pairs of witches, these cards are paired as shown by the numberings they bear in the figure. Here the client represents the thirteenth who rules over the coven. There are a number of more complicated coven methods that need not be described here. Suffice it to say that if necessary each method can be repeated three times, in which case the first is for the past, the second for the present, and the third for

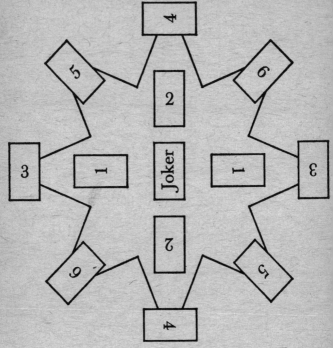

Figure 4.   The Coven of Thirteen

the future. When the seer has mastered this method she will be ready to tackle deeper revelations to be drawn from the use of the Tarots.

The following is an example of a reading using the Star Method. The client this time is not a woman, but a handsome though rather sinister-looking man in his early thirties. The seer chooses the King of Spades to represent him and proceeds according to the rules for this method.

Let us suppose that the three cards exposed by the first three cuts are: the *Page of Clubs*, the *Ten of*

Spades, the *Ten of Clubs*. What do these signify? 'You have just had a message the tone of which I do not like,' says the seer. 'It is full of deceit. Beware. Trust no one until your fortune changes for the better. Then the inheritance that you await will come. The unhappy mental state in which you at present find yourself will have lifted by then. A friend you despise will prove his worth.'

Now the seer makes the Star and reads its packs one by one.

Pack 1: the *Two of Clubs*, the *Page of Hearts*, the *Eight of Hearts*. 'You are a lone wolf, I see, and have encountered much opposition and you are unsettled,' continues the seer, 'perhaps a refugee? Afraid of the Law? I am not quite sure about your relationship with the young man I see here. He amuses you but also annoys you by his free and easy behaviour. However, for the present, you need to be taken out of yourself and he leads you into gay company where you enjoy a harmless flirtation.'

Pack 2: the *Ace of Diamonds*, the *Four of Hearts*, the *Three of Hearts*. 'A letter with news of great importance is on the way,' says the seer. 'I am not sure about the engagement you have in mind. You are too anxious to prove yourself through marriage. You are panicky and that is why you have to consult me today.'

Pack 3: the *Four of Clubs*, the *Page of Diamonds*, the *Six of Clubs*. The seer ponders a while and then says, 'Take care, danger ahead, be careful whom you trust. Ah, the Page of Diamonds, I don't think I trust him!

If you concentrate more on your business and less on such loose company, after all, I think it would be better for your future. Yes, you will succeed where the heart is concerned. Not just at present I fear.'

Pack 4: the *Page of Clubs* (who appeared in the first cut of three piles), the *King of Spades*, the *Queen of Spades*. 'Take a young and integral partner into your firm or political party or whatever your profession is,' the seer says. 'You have either got to sack that worthless underling or so discipline him that he turns over a new leaf. You like being a dictator so go ahead, isn't that how it is?'

Pack 5: the *Three of Clubs*, the *Five of Clubs*, the *Nine of Clubs*. 'Ah, a preponderance of Clubs,' the seer grunts. 'A long partnership later, and one day, a rich marriage, yes. Not bad for the future. It's the present that I don't like. Lone wolf. Ah well, no harm for the moment but let me tell you, the way you drive your car is shocking!'

Pack 6: the *Eight of Clubs*, the *Seven of Clubs*, the *Five of Diamonds*. The seer admonishes 'Never gamble. Avoid lotteries. Take care over borrowing. There are those who will back you financially, never fear. There you are again, dominated by that older woman, did I mention that before? Could be your mother. I can't say for sure. Later in life that marriage. Ambition comes first with you. How fickle you can be and not only with the fair sex but with your colleagues. Honesty is the best policy. You don't believe me, my friend, but really that is true.'

Pack 7: the *King of Diamonds,* the *Eight of Spades,* the *Ace of Spades.* 'Here is a ruthless man highly placed who has an eye on your career, but take care. You go on an important mission. Fear will get you nowhere. I see much intrigue,' the seer says hesitantly. 'There is death. It is not you, but so near, very near. Strengthen your character. Such a career ahead of you if you can master your own weaknesses.'

Pack 8: the *Three of Spades,* the *Two of Diamonds,* the *Six of Hearts.* 'I am looking far ahead,' the seer says, 'there is street fighting. You rise to power. I see it all. What success. What intrigue. That fine house and the grand marriage ... but then the tears. Yes, you will look back and see the heart that you have broken. Your own heart will at last begin to ache. Is it all worth it, sir? Stop and think *now.* The fates can be wooed, destiny may change. We have to believe that which we do. Change now, seek another path, triumph over your weaknesses. Yes, you have it in you to be more noble than your cards would make you out to be. Surmount your character weaknesses. *This you know you can do.'*

And now the seer recapitulates, modifying where she feels it necessary to do so, strengthening the client with positive suggestions, and it is to be hoped, sending him away a wiser and perhaps a better man than when he came to seek her wisdom.

2

Taromancy: The Art of Tarot Card Divination

How to tell fortunes with the Tarot cards is a more serious matter than doing so with ordinary playing cards. The Tarots have a special magic of their own as any sensitive person who has handled a pack can perceive, and as the trained occultist knows full well. The profundity of meaning hidden within their symbol-pictures is great indeed. They are not only a means of divination but hold under glyph, sign and sigil, the secret doctrine of the magi. They could be likened to an encyclopedia of occult philosophy, psychology, science and religion. They should be treated with awe, affection and respect.

A full pack is composed of a greater arcana holding twenty-two Initiation image picture and trance awakening cards, which is supported by a lesser arcana of sixteen court cards – Kings, Queens, Knights and Pages – and forty 'pip' cards.

The four suits of the lesser arcana are: *Cups* corresponding to *Hearts*; *Swords* corresponding to *Spades*; *Platters* corresponding to *Diamonds*; *Wands* corresponding to *Clubs*.

THE TWENTY-TWO GREATER ARCANA

Zero. The Fool. *Le Mat.* Everyman on the Life Path. Folly.

I. The Juggler or Magus. *Le Bateleur.*	Choice.
II. Pope Joan. *La Papesse.*	Secret Doctrines.
III. The Empress. *L'Impératrice.*	Intuition.
IIII. The Emperor. *L'Empereur.*	Reason.
V. The Pope. *Le Pape.*	Inspiration.
VI. The Lovers. *L'Amoureux*	Love sacred and profane.
VII. The Chariot. *Le Chariot.*	Success. Travel.
VIII. Justice. *La Justice.*	Equilibrium.
VIIII. The Hermit. *L'Hermite.*	Sagacity.
X. The Wheel. *La Roue de Fortune.*	Fate. Chance.
XI. Strength. *La Force.*	Courage.
XII. The Hanged Man. *Le Pendu.*	Sacrifice.
XIII. Death (unnamed on the card as a rule).	Rebirth.
XIIII. The Angel. *Tempérance.*	Prudence.
XV. Satan. *Le Diable.*	Temptation.
XVI. The Tower struck by Lightning. *La Maison Dieu.*	Change.
XVII. The Star. *L'Etoile.*	Initiation. Good luck.
XVIII. The Moon. *La Lune.*	Danger. Instability.
XVIIII. The Sun. *Le Soleil.*	Joy. Union.

XX. The Last Judgment.   Total
     Le Jugement.   assessment.
XXI. The World. *Le Monde.*   Triumph.

The numerical order of the greater arcana varies according to the teachings given in different lodges. The old French titles and numbering are added here as they appear on the *Tarot de Marseille*, used mostly by the gypsies. A key word or two as to divinatory meaning is given for easy reference. The suits of the ordinary playing cards may be consulted for an interpretation of the lesser arcana as they hold a corresponding meaning. It should be mentioned that the Pages may represent either youths or maidens, or boy or girl children. The Knights of the Tarot pack give more scope in choice and description of persons. The greater arcana as a method of Initiation is explained in Part Three.

MODUS OPERANDI: THE TREE OF LIFE

THE CABALISTIC METHOD

Here, the seer shuffles the full Tarot pack, cuts it in two, turns the bottom half upside down, then rejoins it with the top half and again shuffles. This ensures that all previous fluids, astral dregs, or personal magnetism left in the cards by previous clients, is exorcised. Also that a number of the cards that have an upright or 'head and feet' appearance will, when disclosed later, be revealed with the images reversed, standing on their heads as it were. This is an important operation on the part of the seer, for a different interpretation results from an upright or a reverse appearance.

The client is now instructed to shuffle and to cut the full deck into three piles with the left hand, placing these face downwards on the table. The seer turns these three piles upwards and consults the three top cards they show. Each is read separately and then in conjunction. The cards are now gathered into one pack again and the client is asked to reshuffle them. When this has been done thoroughly, the seer takes back the pack and constructs the Tree of Life which is derived from the charts and teachings of the Cabalists (see Figure 5).

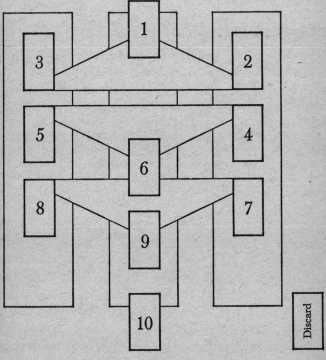

Figure 5.   The Tree of Life

The Tree of Life is composed of ten piles of seven cards each – face downwards until the seer turns them face upwards for the reading. The remaining cards are placed in a separate pack away from the Tree and to the right of the seer to be used for additional clarifications at the end of the reading if necessary. Starting from pile number 1 and continuing through to pile number 10 the seer uncovers each set of sevens in turn, reads these cards separately and then in conjunction and finally making a synthesis of all seventy cards as they are now exposed face upwards upon the Tree.

By studying the figure it will be seen that the Tree is composed of three pillars: *The Pillar of Harmony* in the centre, *The Pillar of Love* on the right and *The Pillar of Discipline* on the left.

The ten packs that are under the influences of the ten Sephirah who rule over these ten centres of power upon the Tree are as follows:

Pack 1. At the summit of the Pillar of Harmony. Holding the meaning, idealism.

Pack 2. At the summit of the Pillar of Love. Holding the meaning, wisdom.

Pack 3. At the summit of the Pillar of Discipline. Holding the meaning, knowledge.

Pack 4. At the middle of the Pillar of Love. Holding the meaning, charity.

Pack 5. In the middle of the Pillar of Discipline. Holding the meaning, severity.

Pack 6. In the centre of the Pillar of Harmony. Holding the meaning, sacrifice.

Pack 7. At the bottom of the Pillar of Love. Holding the meaning, triumph.

Pack 8. At the bottom of the Pillar of Discipline. Holding the meaning, fame.

Pack 9. On the Pillar of Harmony below pile 6. Holding the meaning, solidity.

Pack 10. At the bottom of the Pillar of Harmony. Holding the meaning, realisation.

It will be noticed that the piles on the Tree form at the topmost an upright triangle; one below the other under this, two downward pointing triangles. These are named, respectively, the spiritual triangle, the intellectual triangle, and the intuitional triangle. These influences must be sought in those cards that fall upon them.

The names of the pillars and the triangles, and the hint at a general meaning for each pile built on the pattern of the Tree, will give the seer an indication of the cards as they are revealed in these positions.

For a first session, if the client requires a thorough reading and not an amusing superficial wish-fulfilment one, the Tree may be built three times; first for past, secondly for the present, and thirdly for the future, which is an arduous and lengthy process. To ease the strain of such a clairvoyant *tour de force* a session on three consecutive days can be adopted – one in which the clairvoyant unveils and explains the history of the client up to the present, one given over to immediate problems and possibilities, and one in which the clairvoyant outlines the future, warns of coming dangers and shows future successes and joys. Reading the past includes not only an account of the past life of the client but a description of inherited traits, the *karmic* results of past incarnations, character formation as a result of environment or the pressure of society – in fact the seer will present the client with a detailed analysis, showing where faults of character and past mistakes can be corrected and overcome in future, as well as a description of gifts that may be further exploited or developed. We could call this an occult psychoanalysis.

Reading the present, the seer will describe the immediate situation of the client himself, the emotional tone of his reactions, the characters of the people surrounding him in his home and at work, his love life, and his hopes and fears. This could be called an occult existentialist approach. If necessary illnesses may be diagnosed and the client directed to the appropriate medical specialist for treatment. Great care and a sense of responsibility is required here, for the seer is probably not a doctor and should not suggest remedies for anything more serious than, say, the common cold.

Reading the future which unfolds from what has been learned concerning the past and present, the seer will chart the coming years with the rise and fall of good or bad luck, explain the nature of the ceaseless change that is the rhythm of manifest life. The seer will show where danger threatens, give advice as to how such dangers lying ahead may be avoided, or courageously faced and surmounted. The client will be urged to become positive if he is negative, to break confining habits and make, if needed, radical changes in his daily life. There will be words of consolation, admonishment, and sage advice. Of such is the occult art of divining by means of the magic of the Tarot. The seer will pay attention to the spiritual needs of the client – the highest triangle; to his reasonable demands and practical or objective problems – the midmost triangle; and to his sensitive, vibratory, and intuitive self – the lowest triangle. At the root of the Tree is the tenth position. This concerns the fullest descent into matter of the spiritual or God-nature in man. It conceals the portal to the underworld, the shadow side of every man's nature. Only the most highly-trained, magically well-protected, and spiritually advanced or pure seer should ever cross this threshold and explore the realms of Hades.

THE DIVINATORY SIGNIFICANCE OF THE TWENTY-TWO GREATER ARCANA

Zero. *The Fool, Joker* or *Vagabond Gypsy; Le Mat* or *le Fou*. Man in his folly bent on adventure – everyman on the life path. The basic instincts. Material existence. Man nostalgic for, or fearful of, the past, heedless of the dangers ahead. Befriended by his faithful dog he seeks the butterfly that is his soul or higher self, or stoops to worldly fortune, the golden ball at his feet. If heaven is in the sky above him, his feet stumble among the flowers and thorns of mother earth while in a yawning crevice before him lurks a crocodile representing the mouth of hell. If he is like the ragged gypsy the dogs bark at his heels and stones are thrown by the mob. This is the image card of flesh and blood. *In reverse:* refusal to face life, to accept both the light and the dark of life.

I. *The Juggler* or *the Magician; Le Bateleur* or *le Marge*. The power of the will. Freedom of choice. To gamble with one's life. To be a trickster and deceiver or to devote all to study, to serious pursuits, to seek wisdom and the spiritual life. This is the image card of the rational body. *In reverse:* lack of orientation, discontent and avarice.

II. *Pope Joan* or *the High Priestess; La Papesse* or *la Porte du Sanctuaire.* Occult training or teaching. Thought. But also ambition. For the wise; silence and discretion. The power of the mother image. This is the image card of the spiritual self. *In reverse:* passivity, procrastination. A secretive nature.

III. *The Empress; L'impératrice* or *Isis-Uranie.* Action. Fecundity. Tenderness. Luxury. Creativity. The image card of generation. *In reverse:* dissension, argumentation, ill-health. Confusion.

IIII. *The Emperor* or *the Grand Master; L'Empereur* or *La Pierre Cubique.* Success. Realisation of an important goal. Gifts. Dignity. The image card of royalty. *In reverse:* danger. Be on the alert. Tears. Persecution. Weakness. Vulgarity.

V. *The Pope* or *Hierophant; Le Pape* or *Le Maître des Arcanes.* Inspiration. Philosophy. Transmission of the ancient wisdom. Rest. The image card of traditionalism. *In reverse:* danger. Be on the alert. Tears. Persecution. Weakness. Sloth.

VI. *The Lovers* or *the Two Paths; L'Amoureux* or *Les Deux Routes.* Love sacred or profane. Passion. Sensuality. The appetites. Indulgence. Choice between a simple love or a rich marriage. Also between love for the opposite sex or love for wisdom. A normal or a perverse love. The image card of the passional self. *In reverse:* disorder. Divorce. Indecision. Perplexity. Over-indulgence.

VII. *The Chariot* or *Caravan; Le Chariot* or *Le Char d'Osiris.* Victory. Righteous anger. Journeys. A prize. Fame. Exploration. The image card of the nomadic character. *In reverse:* accidents. Bad news. Delay. Lack of direction. A goal unrealised.

VIII. *Justice; La Justice* or *La Balance et le Glaive.* Balance. Harmony. Legal rights. A test. A high position. The image card of cosmic rhythm and individual equilibrium. *In reverse:* a miscarriage of justice. Prison. Unbalanced force.

VIIII. *The Hermit* or *Seer; L'Hermite, le Capucin* or *La Lampe Voilée.* The search for the truth. Wisdom. Austerity. Ethics. Old age. The image card of he who seeks to listen to the inward voice. *In reverse:* a traitor or false teacher or friend. Conspiracy. Controversy. Political unrest.

X. *The Wheel of Fortune* or *the Sphinx; La Rove de Fortune* or *Le Sphinx.* Success. Renown. Riches. Ambition. Faith and luck. The humble replace the mighty ones. The image card of destiny. *In reverse:* bad luck. Fall from power. Instability. Change. Mystification.

XI. *Strength* or *the Lion Tamer; Le Force* or *Le Lion Muselé.* Health. Strength. Domination. Peace triumphing over violence. The image card of occult power. *In reverse:* illness. Weakness. Error. Enslavement. Decadence.

XII. *The Hanged Man* or *the Sacrifice; Le Pendu* or *Le Sacrifice.* Persecution. Patience. Bravery. Daring.

Unconventionality. Apparent perversity. The image card of spiritual man crucified in matter. *In reverse:* crime. Punishment. Discouragement. A severe illness. Pain.

XIII. *Death* or *Time; La Mort* or *Le Squelette.* Creation. Transformation. Resurrection. Rebirth. Through death to immortality. The image card of the transmutation of a base to a noble character. *In reverse:* long life. Equality. Material success. Survival.

XIIII. *Temperance* or *the Angel; La Temperance* or *Les Deux Urnes.* Initiative. Rhythm. Abundance. Modesty. Sustained strength. Good health. The image card of relationships or correspondences. *In reverse:* trouble. Poverty. Waste. Hesitation. Discord.

XV. *The Devil* or *Baphomet; Le Diable* or *Le Typhon.* Fatality. The arts. Eloquence. Money. Sexuality. Fertility. Magic. The image card of duality or the opposites. *In reverse:* morality. Virtue. Normality. Health restored.

XVI. *The Tower struck by Lightning; La Maison-Dieu* or *La Tour Foudroyée.* Change of roof over the head. Ruin. Fall from power. Distress. Earthquake or other natural cataclysm. The image card of re-orientation or conversion. *In reverse:* a change for the better. Worthwhile risks. Freedom.

XVII. *The Star, the Source; L'Etoile des Marges.* Initiation. Hope. Beauty. Learning. Fame. Imagination. The image card of destiny. *In reverse:* failure. Disharmony. Ignorance. Ill-health.

XVIII.*The Moon* or *the Scarabaeus; La Lune* or *Le Crepuscule.* Dreams. Illicit love. Creativity. Occult choice between the Right and the Left Paths. Genius or insanity. The image card of the etheric body and the astral world. *In reverse:* base passions. A troubled conscience. Neuresthenia. Weaknesses overcome.

XVIIII. *The Sun* or *the Twins; Le Soleil* or *La Lumière Resplendissante.* Happiness. Glory. Triumph of reason. Union of souls. Clarity. Friendship. Duality overcome. The image card of mergence. *In reverse:* adversity. Obscurity. Indecision. Contrariety. Degradation.

XX. *The Day of Judgment; Le Jugement* or *Le Reveil des Morts.* Awakening. Rebirth. Assessment. A fresh start. Reunion. The image card of reincarnation. *In reverse:* false judgments. Errors. Stagnation. Decay. Disillusionment.

XXI. *The World; Le Monde* or *La Couronne des Marges.* Success achieved. Rewards. Visions. Travel. The goal is reached. Glory. The image card of total reintegration. *In reverse:* cataclysms. Failure. Doom. Falseness. Delusions. Despair.

Only these brief indications of the divinatory meaning of the greater arcana are possible here. The serious searcher after their prophetic and initiatory messages must make a study of each image card at great length, and not only consult such books on the Tarot as he may be able to find, but to discuss if possible, variations of symbolism and significance with both wandering gypsy master and learned initiates throughout the world –

not forgetting the humble witch with her intuitive knowledge of these matters.

The following is a short indication of how a reading by means of the Tree of Life method might appear. For this purpose the seer will take only three cards from each of the ten piles on the Tree and interpret each card separately and then make a summary to conclude the consultation. We will assume the client to be a fair-complexioned, attractive but nervous woman – this was clearly emphasised by the appearance of the Queen of Platters when she made the preliminary three cuts for the seer.

Pack I in the First Sphere. Nine of Cups reversed. *The Lovers (VI). Ace of Cups* reversed. The seer intent upon the cards says, 'I can see, madame, that you have suffered great misfortune and you feel broken in mind and body. But these Cups bring peace and quiet. They pour blessings down upon you, but you must seek greater sincerity in your personal relationships. Make a wish now and it will be fulfilled. You need no proof that you are loved, for he who guards your heart is faithful to you. The rich marriage that you made stands between you and your lover. You are anxious both to keep your wealth and yet to give your heart more fully. I see that you are already a widow. Changes are on the way. Be patient, for in a short while you will marry again. Please do not protest, madame, this gypsy always knows what is sure to come to pass.'

Pack II in the Second Sphere. Three of Platters. Knight of Wands. Three of Cups. 'Separation from your first husband could have led to divorce but he was not young and died but recently. He was a stern but fine man and you miss his down-to-earth wisdom. Patience. You will be taken care of again. You are so impetuous and yet so often undecided. Your unwise behaviour may cause scandal.'

Pack III in the Third Sphere. Nine of Wands. Temperance (XIIII). *Ace of Wands* in reverse. 'This is not the time to quarrel with your friends. Wait, a change of luck is on the way. Again I say – patience. If you can allow nine months to pass away, then will be the moment for you to take the initiative. Moderation now. I don't like to see your finances disappearing. Are you extravagant? I think so. Misfortune lies there.'

Pack IV in the Fourth Sphere. The Fool in reverse. *The Tower* (XVI) in reverse. *Knight of Swords.* 'This is no time to be foolish. Stay quietly in your home. It is not the prison you think it is. You will soon see the one you love rising to fortune. He has been poor until now but he will conquer all obstacles and become very successful. He has a soldierly nature and is very chivalrous.'

Pack V in the Fifth Sphere. The Judgment. The Emperor (IIII) in reverse. *Ten of Cups* in reverse. 'All will be well, all will be new. A fresh start awaits you. Free from the demands of a noble but sick man – your former husband no doubt – blessings rain down upon you. Your finances will be even better than before. What unexpected good luck! What success will be yours! Soon you will be able to express yourself in the way you have dreamed. You are interested in entertaining and amateur dramatics, I see.'

Pack VI in the Sixth Sphere. Page of Swords. Pope

Joan (II) in reverse. *Eight of Platters.* 'I mentioned scandal or gossip, I believe. Here I see a young man whose looks I don't like at all. He is lazy and treacherous and exploits people. You lent him some money he won't pay back. Show him the door, madame, when next he comes to see you. He offered you financial advice, even placed some money for you. You were easily tempted. . . . In eight or nine months you will be rested enough to take a pleasant journey which you long for. The one you love will meet you at the end of that voyage. You will find it all . . . ah! Such an adventure!'

Pack VII in the Seventh Sphere. Eight of Wands in reverse. *King of Platters* in reverse. *Seven of Swords* in reverse. 'Friends gather round you, you are very popular. However, do not make too many demands on them. And avoid the gambling table for a while. I can see that you are very fond of a flutter, my dear. Gambling is a vice, you know. No real success lies in that direction. Of course this gypsy can give you a few lucky numbers, but not until your luck shows signs of really changing for the better. It is time to improve relations with your family. I know that you are criticised for your seemingly hard nature where they are concerned. And you must not bicker with that nice young man of yours – not so young you say? He has to work hard towards success. I have promised you that he will be waiting for you at the finale of that delightful journey, about the end of the year.'

Pack VIII in the Eighth Sphere. Queen of Cups. Five of Cups. King of Cups. 'What an extraordinary run of Cups, madame! Look, the Queen, the Five and the

King. What could be better? I saw you as the Queen of Diamonds but now I see a marvellous change and you become the Queen of Hearts. Oh, I am so happy for you! Overcome your hesitation to make a choice. Be decided in future. You are decided where money is concerned but so undecided in this matter of the heart. I have told you what a splendid and successful man your lover will become – and shortly too. More quickly than I at first expected.'

Pack IX in the Ninth Sphere. Five of Swords. Justice (VIII) *reversed. The Moon* (XVIII). 'Here we come to the happy marriage after a long delay, Madame, and great achievements for you, probably in the arts. For your future husband, in connection with the army. Legal matters come right; past mistakes are corrected. Your morbid anxieties give place to lovely dreams fulfilled. Your new home will be built upon a solid foundation.

Pack X in the Tenth Sphere. Three of Wands. The Star (XVII). *Queen of Swords.* 'Yes, your re-marriage is a sure success. It will endure for the rest of your life. Your Star is in the ascendant. Worries and troubles are behind you. What you do not expect is the arrival of three children. Yes, I know it is getting late for that but so it will be. Can I say fairer than that, Madame? I rejoice on your behalf.'

What the seer has not said is that the Star and the Queen of Swords were in reverse until quickly turned by the wise gypsy, the right way up. The fact is that the client will retain her mischief-making and spiteful nature but change, we must believe, is always possible, transformations can come about. With the positive suggestions of the seer, things may improve as time goes on. It should be noted that time and quantity are represented by the number of 'pips' on a card.

SOME HINTS FOR THE FORTUNE TELLER

Apart from a profound knowledge of the cards, the meanings of which can only be suggested in lists such as those in this book, the seer must have a psychological understanding of the character traits and the problems of the clients who seek a consultation and an ethical code or philosophy – not necessarily conventional or orthodox – by which to guide their actions when possible. And, above all, a cultivated and heightened intuition which, added to an inborn gift of clairvoyance, make of the good seer more than just an entertaining and superficial reader of the cards. The seer need not rely only on the cards, but may support his or her revelations by resorting to other means of divination such as the use of the crystal or the study of the hands. Positive suggestion is invaluable as an aid to healing the body and overcoming any morbidity of the mind. It can also give strength to the faint-hearted – for faint heart never won fair lady! Care should always be taken not to instil fear or encourage a superstitious attitude towards any method of divination.

The seer must be possessed of good 'patter' for a reading. Certain stock phrases will often help to condense and pinpoint a truth revealed. It is necessary to know when to let words flow easily and with speed, and when to pause impressively and make a slowly thought-out interpretation of a run of cards.

Generally a reading starts rather superficially but deepens as the seer passes into a trance or semi-trance state when contemplating the magical images on the cards. Towards the end of a reading, the seer will be coming out of this trance state and may conclude with a few lively, homely, or humorous words of reassurance. There are exceptions, of course, as the trance may come almost before the cards are laid. It may not come at all, in which case, a simple reading of little importance is given with apologies.

Occasionally there is a fearful moment when the seer feels tongue-tied and unable to say any more. The seer may, perhaps, feel something sinister or overwhelmingly tragic emanating from the cards, and the atmosphere in the room seems charged with disruptive force. Such a moment must be hastily and skilfully dispersed so that it or what it portends is not disclosed to the client. After all, the seer may be wrong in sensing this seeming revelation from beyond, or it may be intended for someone other than the client. The wise magus knows how to interpret and then dispel such dark forces. Naught may hurt him who lives in truth and in light.

3

Initiation by Way of the Tarot of the Bohemians

THE greater arcana of the Tarot represents a Path of Initiation for the gypsy master and his disciples. At least a little knowledge of this Path is essential for the serious reader of the cards.

Each of the image cards are used as a subject for trance-meditation. Skill in entering and emerging from a divinatory trance may be easily acquired by anyone who has the desire to give an in depth reading of the cards.

During such a trance the Tarot images appear to come alive, to act their symbolic roles about the gypsy master's disciple. He, if he passes all the tests successfully, may become a gypsy master in his turn.

The scene for this mystery performance is within the emblematically-decorated gypsy caravan. After explaining to the reader as far as he can and without breaking pledges, the nature of each of the three times seven steps that are the pattern of this Path the writer will give instructions, warnings and an example.

THE PATH OF INITIATION

There are three 'caverns' through which the disciple must pass with honour: the Cavern of the World of Men, the Cavern of the Underworld of Souls and the Cavern of the Holy Hidden World of the Gods. There are seven steps within each cavern. They are numbered and governed according to the cards – from one to twenty-one.

The Zero Card or Fool. This represents the disciple himself coming from the everyday world to enter and travel from cavern to cavern. Bedraggled as he is, he comes dancing in cap and bells. He is Piers Plowman or Everyman, but in the case of the disciple he need not necessarily be the dull clod who stumbles as best he can from the cradle to the grave, not understanding his destiny, driven by his instincts, conditioned by society – in youth, bent on every kind of foolishness, and dragged down by ill health in old age. Instead of accepting these 'inevitables' the would-be disciple, dimly perceiving that life can be other than mere passing pleasure and much sorrow, makes the primal choice of 'being *in* the world but not *of* the world'. Somehow or another, he feels he can be lifted by devotion to the search for knowledge and the practice of virtue, and that he might be able to reach the final achievement of a triumphant spirit, working through matter in an evolutionary cooperation with the Divine. He sees, in a flash of vision, that man is in essence – God. Knowing life and death, good and evil, he will gain the immortality that is rightly his. Welcomed by the gypsy master he enters the Path.

Men may laugh and call him fool when he abandons the riches of this world for the wandering search of a vagabond and gypsy. So begins his great adventure – adventure into truth. Savage dogs may rend his tattered clothes, yet his own faithful hound will follow him devotedly. He sees his soul and its aspirations in the butterfly among the flowers by the wayside, while he kicks afar the golden ball of wealth and fame from under his feet. He risks his all, not in the pitch and toss of a game of chance, but by the magic wand of faith that is his staff. The risk is fearsome, for he may yet fall headlong into the pit that yawns before him where the 'monster of delusion' opens its crocodile jaws ready to devour him. He holds his head high, gazing at the passage of sun, moon and stars. He is about to take the first step into the Cavern of the World of Men in which he will encounter and, it is to be hoped, overcome the illusions of a worldly life.

Various dilemmatic proposals will be presented to him on the Path and he, in his turn, will participate in making choices among these, choosing rightly or wrongly, failing or succeeding as the case may be. The images of the Tarot, come to life, will act their parts and play this game of life with him. Filled with pity for himself and compassion for mankind, he will brave all in seeking to *know*.

THE CAVERN OF THE WORLD OF MEN

I. *The First Step governed by the Juggler-Magician. Summa – Infima.* There is always choice upon the Life Path, and every step brings its own choices that must be made. Here the disciple finds himself before a

juggler at a village fair who is the gypsy trickster con-
cealing the master behind his parti-coloured clothes.
How many temptations he presents to the innocent
disciple! A draft from the cup of love that will bring
the satisfaction of the passions, the sword that will
bring conquest of both earthly and demoniacal foes, the
platters of wealth that will ever be filled with bread,
and the wand of power that will ensure domination
over other men. We will suppose that the disciple shuts
his eyes from such illusions. When he opens them
again, the juggler is no longer there. In his place stands
the magician, the master of white and black magic.
This magus is sacrificing before a golden altar. He
speaks in awe-inspiring terms of a deeper choice – that
between the Right-Hand Path or the Left-Hand Path,
between the powers of good and the powers of evil,
between light and darkness. His magic rod acts as a
wand of power between the heavens above and the
earth beneath. He instructs the disciple in the occult
laws of analogy – as above so below, as below so above.
The brim of his cap forms a figure of eight in a hori-
zontal position – a mystic sign signifying that behind
all magical operations is hidden the great sacrifice. It
is the sign of the Messiah to come.

II. *The Second Step governed by the Goddess Isis.*
Anima mundi. The magician has parted the curtains
behind the altar of sacrifice and, in the depths beyond,
the disciple beholds the lady of men's hearts, the queen
both of heaven and fecund earth. Isis enthroned. From
heaven she came to give life to the world, she is Mother
Nature, the power concealed in matter, the warm blood
of life itself. She is the sublime feminine principle, the

matriarch who ruled the civilisations of men of the dawn before the male usurped her throne, and intellect superseded intuition. She is the *anima* in the unconscious of every man, as when she adopts the beard of Osiris, she is the *animus* in the unconscious of every woman. It is she who must be obeyed. She conjures before the eyes of the disciple, visions of the past and of that which is to come. She turns the pages of the *akasic* records from which these visions are drawn. She holds the thread of birth, life, and death. She is the three faces of the moon and is called by her devotees, the Triple Goddess. Could one do other than choose to obey so mighty a divinity?

III. *The Third Step governed by the Empress. Vis Vitae*. Isis has changed herself from an august goddess into the mother of man – the good Eve whose face in reverse is the evil Lilith. She is the goddess Ceres, seen seated in a field of corn by a fall of water. To her all the birds sing. She modifies the cosmic vibrations of the divine effulgence of life according to the evolving needs of this world. By this energy, what we call matter is condensed. She objectifies that which Isis in her mightiness must conceal as the 'unknowable'. Such spiritual energies have their voluptuous aspect as they operate here on the plane of manifestation. The twelve signs of the zodiac are above her head. Concealed by her rich mantle is the secret door to the *Venusburg*-initiation of the passional self. Should the disciple choose happiness in this realm of the senses or must he pass from this Eden to seek a greater bliss elsewhere?

IIII. *The Fourth Step governed by the Emperor. Stabilia Instabilit*. The disciple starts forward as if to throw himself into the arms of Venus but veils fall between him and the goddess. When the magician draws them back again, the Emperor appears seated with legs crossed – the position of the Master Mason – upon a squared and cubed throne beneath the over-shadowing wings of Isis. As her spouse he is the god Osiris, as her brother and her son he is Set and Horus – Set, the Lord of Darkness, and Horus, the incarnate god-king, ruler of mankind. The Emperor holds emblems of spiritual and material power in his hands, the *crux ansata* of virility and the orb of world domin-ion. Does he offer the disciple the kingdoms of this world or the key to the heaven-world of the gods? Here-in lies the choice: Upper or Lower Egypt? All the secrets known as freemasonic are enscribed in hiero-glyphs on the foundation of his throne. This god-king expounds the laws of just government, of husbandry, and craftsmanship. He tells of the sevenfold nature of man and the universe; the bodily, etheric, passional, vital, mental, soul, and spiritual natures that in inte-gration make of man a human-divine entity. Isis gives knowledge through intuition, Osiris-Horus gives it through the intellect. The crossing of the legs is the safeguard against enemies in this world and the dark forces that impel these to cause misery born of ignor-ance.

V. *The Fifth Step governed by the Pope or Hiero-phant. Sacra inflat.* Again the curtains fall and again they part. The Hierophant is seated upon his pontifical throne with his ecclesiastical court about him. Where-as Isis on the cards wore the mask of Pope Joan and held the Book of Thoth – the wisdom of the esoteric

Tarot – so the Hierophant, masked as the Pope, holds the keys of the outer and inner worlds; of the kingdoms in both of which that wisdom holds sway. The choice before the disciple here is between conformity with the acceptance of authority, or non-conformity and the acceptance of the hazards of the search and reliance on the light within. This is the light of the inward god, which can be known by all men who attend to it no matter to which faith they adhere in the outer world. If the disciple chooses the latter Path of self-reliance, self-knowledge and inward guidance, then the mask of Pope is cast aside and the Hierophant is the Friend and not the Dictator of his disciples. That which has been concealed from the ignorant is revealed to him who ever seeks the light.

VI. *The Sixth Step governed by the Lovers. Bivium Vitae*. The disciple falls into a deep sleep and on awakening finds himself in a garden full of flowers where he wanders entranced. Two women approach him. One is a matron, richly dressed; the other a maid in a simple gown. The matron places her hand upon his shoulder and draws him towards her. She proposes marriage to him, and places all her wealth at his disposal. The maiden points her hand toward his heart. She has nothing to offer but her love, her purity, and beauty. He feels that he has been so long in the enchanted cavern among high divinities and admonishing masters that, in the fresh air and perfume of the garden, he is sorely tempted. If the wrong choice is all but made, Eros himself comes to restrain him; the arrow is about to be shot at the disciple and the maid. But what is this? The matron is no longer there and,

in her place, stands a magus who, with stern commands, bids him to follow. Does he falter? Does the
disciple look despairingly towards the maid? Is there
no other way? Perhaps there is.

VII. *The Seventh Step governed by the Lord of the
Chariot. Impera tibi.* All has faded except a road that
winds among the flowers to distant hills. A chariot or
is it a painted caravan that appears, drawn by white
and black horses or sphinxes? Under a multi-coloured
canopy rides the gypsy master himself. So far, the right
choices must have been made, for behold, the disciple
mounts the chariot beside this princely personage and
together they proceed upon the road of triumph. The
Cavern of the World has been left far behind. This is
a moment of truth, a great realisation.

THE CAVERN OF THE UNDERWORLD OF SOULS

VIII. *The Eighth Step governed by the Spirit of
Justice. Acquilibratio Rerum.* The life of the world
the disciple is leaving behind now seems as the winter
months, in which the seeds of the spiritual life have
been sown, only flowering as he rides away. Through
those slumbering months while walking the earth, the
disciple lived, he now sees, as one dead, for he had
slowly transmuted the personal self in separation – the
'I' – and put on his higher individuality, the new man.

   The number eight is that of Justice as when represented horizontally is that of the divine suffering or
imprisoned in matter. At such a deep level, this no
longer signifies for the disciple sacrifice of the personal
flesh to the demands of the spiritual man but instead,

how these two opposites may be equilibrated so that
individual harmony is achieved.

Driving beside the master, confident that he has
passed the seven tests of the First Initiation, the disciple now sees the ground open before them. Leaping
in fear from the chariot, he finds himself alone in the
underworld. Chariot and master, both have disap-
peared. As the eyes of the disciple grow accustomed to
the all-pervading gloom he discerns a vast pair of scales
watched over by a great concourse of spirits. The gods
who judge the dead, Thoth and Anubis, the Lords of
Karma of the Hindus, who are weighing souls against
the lightness of the father of truth. Typhon, the
monster of the deep, awaits below ready to devour
those who are found wanting.

'What choice have I here?' cries the disciple as he is
cast into the scale.

'Do you not know that the soul may choose?' a voice
asks him. 'Is God so lacking in compassion as to con-
demn even the most sinful of his children to an eternity
of torment?'

The Spirit of Grace seems to bear his soul away and,
in those healing arms, he falls asleep.

VIIII. *The Ninth Step governed by the Hermit.*
Secreta Investigat. Refreshed the disciple awakens by
the side of a road that winds among rocks and through
desolate valleys. Prudently he decides to keep to the
road and not to tarry longer by the wayside. After a
while he encounters an old man shielding a lantern
under his cloak, for the night approaches and howling
winds moan through the valley. This sage leans heavily
upon his staff but holds his head high, penetrating the

darkness with piercing eyes. At his feet a serpent coils and uncoils itself – it is his familiar. He is the sage who ever seeks light in darkness, the philosopher who counsels the young, the prophet who warns those who are bent on evil ways. He bids the disciple follow him. This choice is easy for there is no other light to show the way in this place of shadows. With a lighter heart, the disciple continues upon the road with the old man and his serpent.

X. *The Tenth Step governed by the Sphinx and its Wheel of Fortune. Omnia redeunt.* A turn of the road and the hermit points to an enormous wheel that turns ceaselessly. There is no way to pass it but to mount the ascending side and trust that it will be possible to descend on the far side where the road, it is to be hoped, will continue.

'This is the Wheel of Fate, of birth and death and endless rebirth,' the hermit explains to the disciple. 'Watch before you mount it, what do you see?'

'I see animals like monkeys or rabbits struggling up one side, and I see them disappearing into the darkness down the other,' says the disciple.

'Have they not clothes on?' asks the hermit.

'Indeed they have,' is the reply, 'they seem to be dressed in all manner of clothes, some very poorly but others richly.'

The creatures that the hermit is showing to the disciple are the etheric bodies of human beings. Bodies that are polluted by the struggle for power, by ambition, by vanity. Fate lifts up the lowly man who hungers for success and casts down the mighty who have gained it and try to hold on to it. The disciple may choose to be lifted up and cast down so that he can understand and be compassionate towards all conditions of men. The climb makes him dizzy; in falling he nearly loses consciousness. When he has come to his senses he finds himself in a field of asphodel where youths and maidens dance the round of a fairy circle. He has come to the country of the fairy folk who are neither mortal men nor high divinities but a blend of both, living as they do in this half-world of silver shadows. Will the disciple be caught forever in the land of the Shee – the *Sidhe* or the Little Ones and the Lordly Ones? He has the choice.

XI. *The Eleventh Step governed by the Spirit of Fortitude. Vincit virtus.* Leaving the fairy circle with some regret, the disciple takes shelter from an approaching storm within a nearby grotto. A noise as of battle assails his ears. The whole place seems full of strife. Trying to discern the combatants, he thinks he sees a powerfully built naked man, a Hercules in fact, who beats the air with his club. But then he sees a maiden clasping a pillar that splits in two with a resounding crack. But now, the vision now is of a mature woman gently but determinedly prising open the jaws of a lion. A quotation comes into his head, 'Out of the jaws of the lion cometh forth sweetness'. The wise and gentle wisdom of the hermit who has left him must give place to the strength of will of a dedicated master. The choice is between a passive goodness or an active will to good. The balancing of opposites and the founding of stability or equilibrium is the work and a large part of the goal of every master magician.

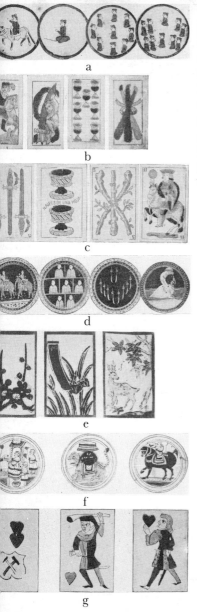

1. A selection of old playing cards. a) Hindu b) Padua c) Spain d) Bombay e) Japan f) Persia g) Early English. These cards were reproduced in an article by J. H. Kemmis entitled 'The Devil's Picture-Books' in *Pearson's Magazine*, Vol 5, 1898.

2. *Above.* *The Card Players* by Michelangelo da Caravaggio. His other works include a painting entitled *Gipsy Fortune Teller.*

3. *Opposite.* A selection of early Tarot cards. a) The Wheel of Fortune, The Tower Struck by Lightning, and The Lovers: Italian Tarot, engraved by C. della Rocca, Milan, 1820. b) The Hanged Man and The Hermit: Italian Tarot, Milan, undated. c) The Fool: an 18th-century Flemish Tarot card.

a

b   c

4. *Above.* Madame Nicole, a present-day Tarot fortune teller.
5. *Opposite.* Trance. *Top left.* Lap man in a trance, with a magic drum on his back, about to foretell the future. *Top right.* A typical illustration of the frenzy Hitler aroused in his followers. *Below.* Kenyan women in religious trance.

6. *Above*. John Dee (1527–1608), thought by many contemporaries to be a charlatan, who became Royal Astrologer and Palmist to Elizabeth I.

7. *Left*. A quiet corner of Chapel Street Market in Islington finds a present-day palmist at work.

The Fortune Teller by Pietro Longli.

9. *Above*. A hoarding in Los Angeles.

10. *Below*. Groups of friends used to gather together for table-tapping sessions. This engraving is dated 1853.

XII. *The Twelfth Step governed by the Hanged Man. Suspensus Inservit.* What is this? The disciple is seized by hooded men and hanged head downwards from a gibbet. He is strung up by one leg so that his other leg bends at the knee, and thus forms the pattern of a cross. His hands are tied behind his back. Gold coins fall from the pockets of his jacket.

'You have not given all,' the hooded ones cry, 'see the gold that showers from your pockets.'

The wretched disciple realises how little, in actual fact, he has abandoned for the Path. Not only has he retained wealth in secret but, and this is far more important, he has held back certain corners of his mind and thus is in danger of tarnishing his soul. He has taken possession of magical powers for personal ends, and has so become enslaved to the magic arts in such a way that he might easily choose the Left Hand Path and plunge to damnation for the space of many existences. But upon the gibbet, he sees the need for a complete sacrifice of the whole self and, confessing himself inwardly to his master, chooses to be the sacrificial victim and not to end a criminal, a deceiver of himself and others. Seeing Death approaching with his scythe, he loses consciousness.

XIII. *The Thirteenth Step governed by Death. Disjungit discrepantia.* The disciple must have been cut down from the gibbet before he was quite dead, for now he is opening his eyes and soon is able to lift his head and look about him. He has been laid upon the marble top of an old tomb in an extensive graveyard. He hears the swishing of a scythe and, fearfully looking in the direction from whence the sound comes, he sees the skeleton Death, reaping among the flowers and grass that almost conceal the many other tombs among which they flourish. But then he sees that it is not flowers that are being mown down, but heads and arms and legs. Some of the bodies to which these belong are half rotted, others mere bones. And then he sees that some of the heads are crowned, some wear mitres, some have 'caps of liberty', others the helmets of soldiers, while yet others must be those of women, for they are elegantly coiffed, others have blossoms, woven with jewels, into fast fading tresses. There are even the heads of little children to be seen. So here is Death, the destroyer of all. Under his scythe must fall the great, the famous, the powerful, the mighty, the tyrant, the rogue, as well as the scholar and the reformer. Nor is the beauty of womanhood spared. Lady or lady's maid, both fall to the scythe, and then the little children.

'What woe is this?' cries the disciple. 'This then is the end of all!' And then a sign is shown him. He sees Death has inadvertently cut off his own right foot with his own sweeping blade. *There is no death.* The flowers and the grasses proclaim it. The reaper himself has shown it. As spring inevitably follows winter, so life must follow death. An eternal resurrection. The choice is ours. We need not die. Perhaps we can hear fate declare, '*You may not die*'.

XIIII. *The Fourteenth Step governed by the Angel of the Vials. Virtutem Infundit.* The hour of transformation has come: to pass from the second to the third cavern. To qualify as a member of the holy hidden world of the gods – Paradise regained or attained! The Cavern of the Earth World has been passed through honourably, the Cavern of the Underworld has been survived.

On this step a transmutation of the earthly and the etheric bodies of the disciple into the spiritual and divine nature must take place. Then the way through the other steps of the third cavern will appear.

Standing at the end of the lane bordered with flowers that leads from the cemetery, perplexed as to where to go next, the disciple is met by the Angel of the Vials who takes his hand and guides him through a little gate towards the last of the caverns of Initiation. They approach a holy well and the Angel purifies the disciple by taking two vials standing on its brink and pouring clear water from one to another above his head. The virtue of temperance never allows one or other of these vials to contain more or less, miraculously both hold a like measure and are never empty.

'Draw near,' the Angel says, 'and take from me the vial that pleases you the better. Behold one is of moon iron and the other of sun gold.'

'I will take neither the one vial nor the other,' he says, 'but I will have both if you will give me leave to take them.'

The final test on leaving the second cavern is passed, for nothing in separation is acceptable on the Path. The light and the dark must be harmonised, good and bad vanish away. Both base metal and gold are needed for the alchemical change. Beyond the opposites the truth resides.

'How wise you have become, my friend,' says the Angel with a sad smile, 'now leave this land of shadows and see if your new found wisdom will serve you in the beguiling land that lies ahead of you.'

THE CAVERN OF THE HOLY HIDDEN WORLD

XV. *The Fifteenth Step governed by the Devil or Secret Master. Simia Dei.* The moon sails clear in the heavens above. The disciple finds himself standing before a low hill, gently rounded and covered with short grass. Into this hill opens the door to the third cavern if he can find it. The night air is still, and suddenly there is wafted to him as from a distance but gradually coming nearer, the sound of fairy music – eerie and yet persuasive. When the music is all about him yet no hand seeming to make it, he is drawn to follow it and it leads him to a low stone portal – the entrance to the fairy mound. He remembers nostalgically the fairy circle that he left some long while ago. He longs to enter the hill, to join the merry-makers that he feels must be within. He chooses to enter and the door of stone rolls back upon invisible hinges. The disciple walks into the inside of the hollow hill. He is in the hidden world through which lies the path to Final Initiation.

The hollow hill is walled with blocks of carved stone. A feast is taking place. A number of the fairy folk, of which some are enormously tall and others quite small, dance forward to lead him to their King who is seated seemingly above a cauldron surveying contentedly the ring of sprites that circle before him. The disciple approaches.

'Is this the Devil?' he asks himself.

The King of this coven appears to be human from the waist upwards but goat-like below. He is naked and of splendid form. From his head grow horns between which a tongue of fire flickers. The disciple cannot but notice that the breasts of his Satanic Majesty are almost feminine while between his shaggy thighs an exaggerated phallus rises.

'Am I to choose Lucifer rather than his one-time lord who is my God?' the disciple asks himself. 'Am I to choose the perverse world of fairy rather than the crystal clarity of Heaven? Is Lucifer the true God and Jehovah an usurping demon?'

The answer to these most pertinent questions must remain unwritten and untold. We will suppose that the disciple, after some dallying in these fascinating lands and no doubt learning many strange, perverse, but also wise things while so doing, passes on his way. A mighty crash of thunder and the hollow hill must have vanished for the disciple felt himself falling . . .

XVI. *The Sixteenth Step governed by the Tower. Cave Superbiam.* He had fallen. He lay bruised upon the ground. Thunder rolled and lightning flashed while hail stones rained about him. Through the darkness of the storm he saw a high tower struck. Its crenellated summit was breaking into pieces, and the stones of which it was built were hurled downwards. And from the parapet, two men seemed thrown to certain death below. From one there fell a golden crown, from the other, a fool's cap.

'Nothing to choose between either of them,' came the unbidden thought. As the disciple emerges from this vision and gets up from the ground where he had been prostrated he sees two small pebbles lying at his feet. On an impulse he picks them up. They are pleasant to the touch. He puts them in his pocket and stumbles as fast as his legs will carry him away down the road that leads from the foot of the tower. The meaning of these stones nor the choice attached to them, is not revealed.

XVII. *The Seventeenth Step governed by Star. Superum Influx.* The disciple wanders beside a cool stream, flowing from distant mountains. The storm has passed. He strips off his clothes and plunges into the icy water and then, refreshed, he falls asleep among the rushes that border the stream. When he awakens evening is upon him. In the twilight he sees a naked and lovely maiden kneeling with her left knee upon the bank and her right foot in the water. From two ewers she pours the waters of life to mingle with the waters of the stream. A nightingale sings from a tree nearby, the song tells of hope, of triumph, and of love. The stars come out one by one in the darkening sky. Brighter than all the other stars is Venus-Lucifer, the evening and the morning star, the Star of Initiation. The waters of life flow eternally from the ewers of the maiden mingling with the waters of the world in which the disciple has been cleansed. The star blazes forth its message: the disciple has been chosen by it from the beginning. With a surpassing joy filling his heart, he continues on his way.

XVIII. *The Eighteenth Step governed by the Moon. Regina animarum.* The path leads towards the mountains. It passes a deep pool, and continues between two fierce dogs. To the right and to the left stand two towers. In the depths of the pool the disciple sees a strange crustacean. Is it a crab, lobster, crayfish, scor-

pion, or scarabaeous? Or again, it may be a water
snake. Psychoanalysts will know it as the archetype of
the deep unconscious that is rising to surface consciousness. It can either overthrow the balance of the mind,
fill it with nothing but fantasy and unfulfilled dreams
and wishes, or it can achieve union with the archetypes
of the heights – the patterns designed by the great
architect of the universe upon which manifest life is
being fashioned.

The moon sheds a silver light over the pool, the
path, the dogs that bay at it and snap at the legs of the
disciple who must pass between them, and on the
towers. The disciple, trembling with fear, manages to
pass between the two beasts that seem more like wolves
than dogs, but is tempted to take refuge in one or other
of the crenellated towers. His brow is covered in sweat,
but cool dewdrops fall from the full moon and he is
refreshed. He curbs his desire to take refuge and stead-
fastly marches forward towards the distant hills. He has
understood both the lunatic danger of the pool as well
as its luna qualities of creativity, for it is the reflection
below of the powers of the celestial orb in the night
sky. Having left the baying hounds behind him, he
now knows them to be but chimeras, shadows without
substance. He is thankful that he did not hide within
one or other of the towers, which are really there to
entice the weary seeker away from the portals to the
garden of the sun that lie still far away, at the foot of
the mountain of the wise. How could he take shelter
in mere outer defences, allowing himself to become a
prisoner of forms and never gaining courage to find
the truth, see the light, experience ultimate bliss?
Beyond the mountains he will behold the sunrise.

XVIIII. *The Nineteenth Step governed by the Sun. Pater Spirituum.* The arduous journey over, the disciple finds himself in a walled garden full of flowers and shaded by many kinds of trees. The sun shines brilliantly, touching all below with its golden rays. Arms about each other's necks, running over the grass-green lawns, are two children. They are twins. May the disciple join them in the relaxation of their innocent and happy play? He goes towards them and with one on either side, he advances to a simple temple that is all but hidden in the depths of the garden. It is here that the mystic marriage takes place, and the disciple becomes clothed with the sun and is infilled with God: God transcendent whose rays descend upon him weaving a garment of light about him; God imminent who, as the light within him, irradiates his whole being. The twins are his witnesses.

Now clothed in glory, he stands forth as one fully initiated. Has he conquered all the perils on the way? Yes. But is it ever possible to conquer all the perils that lurk within the self? Perils ever ready to destroy. An Initiate must pass to far greater judgments than ever a disciple has to meet.

XX. *The Twentieth Step governed by the Angel of the Last Trump. Verbum Vivificans.* The face of the sun is obscured. Thunder rolls across the sky and lightning flashes. The trees bend in the storm and the blossoms in the garden are blown away. The sound of a trumpet is heard and the Angel of the Last Day appears. Mighty in stature, of many wings and eyes, he rides upon the clouds awakening the sleeping dead with blasts from his brazen horn. The disciple, now an Initiate, finds that the garden has changed into a tomb from which, naked, he seems drawn upwards by the power of the angelic presence. Cold as the dead whom he sees rising from their graves on every side, he is abject with fear. But he has his sponsors on either side of him ready to testify in his favour. They are the twins now grown to the stature of the masters of life and death who ever assure the miracle of resurrection. Now if the Initiate is found wanting, he will be cast into the pit for re-moulding, and then will start again on the lengthy journey of many transmigrations. For the failure of an Initiate is great indeed. Having become a son of the sun, if the Initiate turns away and chooses the darkness, he then is guilty of the sin of sins. But now he knows the nature of the mirage of ever-changing worlds – be it the earth world, the astral world, the heaven world, or the world of hell itself. All these worlds are true as long as they are thought to be true, all are seen as the flux of life once the third eye of the Initiate is open. Just as there is no death, so there is no eternity of hell or of heaven, but an unnameable, indescribable, state of bliss. The Angel of the Judgment now bestows that bliss upon him.

XXI. *The Twenty-first Step governed by the World Spirit. Mundus Mendax.* Can the disciple, who is now the Initiate, abide forever in that bliss beyond description? Has he reached the end of the Path? He has won the right to merge forever in the shoreless sea of the divine mind. One last choice and the reward could be his.

Where the Angel was, the Initiate now sees a beautiful naked woman garlanded with flowers. Her right foot lightly touches the earth, her left is raised, for she is dancing. In the cross thus formed by her graceful limbs is the sign of sacrifice similar to the one he made when hanging by the foot from the gibbet. But here it is the soul of our earth which has clothed itself in matter and who appears as the world mother. In her hands she carries wands of power with which she directs the cosmic rays. A light veil flutters from her shoulders for she is the truth of the world and the whole of the truth, even for the highest Initiate, can never be quite revealed. She comes over the earth with four companions: a youth, an eagle, a bull, and a lion. They guard the four corners of the world for her and for us, her children.

The Initiate knows that the mightiest of all choices lies before him: to enter forever the state of bliss or to remain in the world of men and strive for the well-being of the many, for the saving of the many, in compassion for all living. The choice is his.

4
The Diviner's Art of Trance Meditation

THAT which is invoked by means of the Tarot cards and the other media under consideration in this book, cannot be sensed or seen unless the seer is in a state of some degree of trance. There are different kinds and different levels of trance states, ranging from the only slightly induced to that which borders on the cataleptic. Only a superficial trance is perceptible in a seer telling fortunes with ordinary playing cards – although there can be unexpected exceptions – but when the Tarots are being used, then a much deeper state is to be observed. The overflow from the trance state of the seer is to some extent transmitted to the client if he is at all suggestible. Thus he begins to see a little of what the seer perceives, as the cards appear one after another on the Tree of Life.

The value, as well as the dangers, in inducing or accepting trance states was well known to the ancients. It is known to the seer of today, and perhaps half-consciously used by actors and public speakers as well as doctors, psychotherapists, and dentists, but is all but ignored by the public at large. The experience, if realised at all, is nervously laughed at with scorn.

Commercial advertising, whether those involved know it or not, however, is making use of it all the time.

The neglected potentials of trance usage for a variety of ends may well characterise our educational, criminal, therapeutical, and recreational methods in the near future. As with any gift of nature, use can go hand in hand with misuse. Trance is a factor in psychological warfare, fermentation of a holy war or pogrom, and political indoctrination. It is the 'hidden persuader'. Both the white and the black magician make use of it.

Applied by the individual, trance is an essential for genius. Applied as a cooperative method it can benefit society both in leisure and in work.

There are magi who claim that through trance vision they have been able to see the powers of darkness at war with the powers of light. In addition, the magi have been able to lend their own occult strength to aid these powers – on whichever side they are – in such a dualistic cosmic war!

We speak of the mentally unbalanced as being beside themselves. When we have been in a rage we also say that we were beside ourselves. Or that something overcame us suggesting non-responsibility for our acts. Being temporarily out of one's rational mind is a claim made by one driven on by jealousy – the *crime passionelle*. The artist and the scientist feel and appear obsessed by their work. Lovers are besotted with one another. When in a dark mood we say of such a person, 'We don't know what got into him'. Someone not feeling too well is said to be not quite himself. If we accidentally stub our toe against a table leg or drop a valuable vase we say, 'I don't know what made me do it'. In our dreams we juxtapose all kinds of seemingly unrelated objects and events – a phenomenon exploited by surrealist painters and horror films. In our day-dreams and fantasies there are those that arise spontaneously, and some which we deliberately cultivate and enjoy: the former represents an unconscious trance state; the latter, self-induced trance. The saint in ecstasy is lost to the rational self. A hero in battle carries out feats of valour that are beyond his ordinary strength.

All these kinds of expressions and experiences point to the fact that there is some force different from or greater than the normal senses, and that gives the impression of being outside the self or temporarily in possession of the self. Furthermore, these forces seem to abide within certain objects or in natural phenomena: a tree, rock, or stream, but also in things made by man, such as an idol shrine, rosary, holy medal, or talisman. These forces exist as well within a pack of image-bearing cards.

Primitive people, simple people, children as well as animals, and trained seers, of course, are well aware of this force. Modern civilisation and the exaltation of the rational seems to have dulled this *instinct* to a certain extent. There are many who would question its existence at all, but the sensing of it and through it the sensing of that which is sensed, is a fact. To study the sensing and that which is sensed, this faculty must be given a name. Both for the scientific investigator as well as the practising occultist, this is important if what is discovered concerning it is to be promulgated. It was named the *numen* by the Romans, having the meaning of 'nod', 'nodding', the assent, command, will, or sway

innate in certain things of value, of mystery, awesome
or friendly. Anthropologists generally refer to it by its
Melanesian name – *mana*. American Indians term it
waken, *orenda*, and *manito*. It is a spirit force rather
than an actual spiritual being or god. The *kami* –
including a multiplicity of spirit forces – of the
Japanese seem to be less personalised than the august
gods yet more personalised than just a force, probably
indicating the nature of this power in the clearest way.
Of course man anthropomorphises it as it emanates
from different centres: an olive tree has its nymph, a
brook its undine, a flame its salamander, a cave or pit
its gnome. The Tarot has its numerous images: the
Hand of God on the Aces, royal persons on the court
cards; the great arcana images of Everyman the Fool,
beautiful naked male and female angelic beings,
friendly or hostile animals and the Lord of Darkness
and his minions; and over all, the divine power of the
spirit of the Tree of Life which is without human or
animal appearance.

We have spoken of a man's being beside himself
unintentionally, but most men from time to time *in-
tentionally* seek to escape from the bondage of the
rational self: the deliberate use of intoxicants such as
alcohol, tobacco and drugs; also by fasting, sexual con-
tinence or the reverse – the ritual orgy; by means of
religious rites with the use of heady incense, chanting
and magical gestures; by participating in the dance.
Society has tried to control as well as to utilise this need
and its expression through a hierarchically-directed
religion, through the pageantry of royalty, through
seasonally permitted festivals. Of old, the tribe was
kept from undue trance escapism and unintentional

excess by its soothsayer, medicine man, or shaman. Perhaps one of the reasons for the world unrest of the young at present is because old methods for permissive trance have grown outmoded, worn thin, decayed. Their magic no longer works and no new ones of significant value have taken their place save the adoration of the pop artist and group, and mass participation in the rhythmic companionship inspired by these most vital means for the satisfaction of the deeper or more basic needs of human nature. These are not able to be satisfied by the higher rational activities of the evolved mental nature. Such outlets are hardly sufficient for world needs, and older people are little affected by them. The situation could easily degenerate into the kind of mass trance or hysteria typical of tyrannous uprising.

In trance states, the impression is of losing awareness or control of the senses. Investigation into the phenomena of various kinds or degrees of trance reveals that the majority of the sense receptor cells in that area of the brain called the hypothalamus are, as it were, paralysed temporarily, although not all, and not completely. In most trance states, the subject can still respond to words of command and can cooperate in group activities such as ritual dancing. Or again, when the trance is not deep, the subject can interpret the images on cards, the signs formed by tea leaves, coffee grounds, or sand, and see and explain visions in a crystal or bowl of water.

The thalamus is a mass of grey matter lying at the base of the cerebrum which contains terminal and high level centres, both sensory and motor, and so is intimately associated with the emotions. The hypothalamus is the region of the forebrain lying below, the underpart or floor so to speak. It controls our primary drives and basic impulses such as aggression or rage as well as regulating body temperature, thus involving the whole sympathetic nervous system. The pituitary, about which occultists have a number of esoteric teachings, lies below this. They say that the vibrations rising from this stir the pineal gland situated in the mid-brain said to be the organ of the third eye – the median eye of lower vertebrates – and in which Descartes placed the seat of the human soul as it impinged upon its vehicle, the earthly body. The rational scientist would no doubt dismiss such seemingly fanciful notions with a sigh.

Trance is induced by dulling or anesthetising the hypothalamus while stimulating the pituitary so that its vibrations open the pineal 'eye' to a different vision of reality or surreality not apparent to normal perception.

Under normal conditions basic drives incite us to appropriate responses to the messages reaching the hypothalamus from our senses. For example, the need for food, for drink, for sexual discharge – needs arising from the stomach, throat, genitals and transmitted from these centres to the brain which demands attention to them. Of course, stimulants will activate such centres so that they demand more than is essential for their ease: the smell of roasting meat, the taste of a glass of wine, the sight of an attractive body, to mention but a few of such stimulants. The use of drugs, the rhythm of drums, or the uttering of chants are likewise stimulants well known to us. But in trance, some or all of the lines of contact with the brain seem temporarily broken, the messages are not transmitted, the way being somehow blocked. The hypothalamus or controlling centre continues to exist, of course, but in some partial or almost total isolation from the senses.

The question is then: by what agency is the hypothalamus activated when separated from the full range of our senses? It would appear that this question has not so far been satisfactorily answered by science.

For those who are prepared to pose metaphysical answers to such phenomena, the concept of a soul is acceptable. But the soul is sometimes said to be absent during trance, to be journeying elsewhere or inhabiting another body or object. The investigating occultist believes that he has seen another entity or soul take control of a trance subject and speaks of possession. Such an entity, it is claimed, may be of someone dead or at a distance, or again it may be of an angelic or demoniacal nature or some other kind of elemental force. In addition we know through the testimony of poets and artists, actors, or saints and mystics that, while working, they have been possessed, dictated to, instructed, and inspired, by entities other than themselves, entities such as the 'muse' of the poet (the *duende* in Spain), the 'voices' of St Joan, the Mahatmas of Madame Blavatsky, even the voice of God himself as in the case of Moses. Psychologists may speak of the voice of the deep unconscious, or the commands of the suger ego. The religiously-minded may speak of the 'inward light', the 'seed within', the voice of conscience, but while we know intuitively what they mean by these terms, we see that they are naming that which so far is nameless scientifically.

There are many techniques for entering the several different kinds of trance state. Under the following headings a number of requisites are indicated. They concern, for the most part, individual trance practice rather than collective trances.

The Surroundings. These should be of a propitious kind. A quiet room specially set aside and used for no other purpose than those pertaining to the occult arts. Failing this, a shrine placed in a corner of one's room, much as ikons hang with lights before them in Russian or Greek homes. A forest grove, a grotto, a mountain peak or hilltop, a peaceful valley or the border of a lake or by the sea; these are nature's sanctuaries for such practices. Then there are ancient temples or ruins as well as restfully streamlined halls set aside for the quiet hour. It should be mentioned that cemeteries are used by some magicians and are much favoured in the East; however, the writer does not recommend such a lugubrious site.

Clothes. The simplest possible. Light, loose, comfortable garments and footwear are advisable. If the climate and surroundings permit, no clothes at all. There are practices where elaborate vestments are used but these are not our concern in this book.

Position. That known as the Rameses posture in which the subject is seated on a chair with back straight and knees and feet almost together, and with the hands resting palm downwards upon the thighs. The Osiris posture, in which the subject lies on his back, relaxed on a couch, the hands folded on the breast crosswise. Or the Lotus posture in which so many Eastern gods are sculpturally represented. Kneeling, as in prayer, is not as a rule advised. Nor prostrations, for these have other, though related, functions than that of trance.

Accessories. The burning of incense accompanied by soft music; repetitive drum beats or chants; lighted candles or lamps; the use of rosaries or 'worry' beads, and prayer wheels. These and many other such aids to trance meditation may be of use; for some they can be a hindrance.

Talismans. These may be created by the subject himself or adapted from those shown in a book of Seals and Sigils or, again, acquired from a magus, witch, or gypsy. Such designs conform more or less to those Eastern meditation charts called *mandalas*, in which the pattern radiates from the centre in a circular, square, or star formation.

Objects. For a focus upon which the eyes may rest, sacred statues, paintings, emblems such as the wheel of the Buddhists (greater arcana X), or the cross of the Christians (greater arcana XII), or the Seal of Solomon (Greater Arcana XV), may be used. But also a flower or floral arrangement such as the Japanese make so skilfully. Each of the Tarots, especially of the greater arcana, are used in this way.

Breathing Exercises. Gentle and regular breathing is sufficient, but the complicated and efficacious methods known as *prana yoga* can also be adapted if known to the subject.

Recitation. The subject may prepare himself and the atmosphere about him by pronouncing magical formulae if he has been instructed in these. Such invocations correspond to *mantra yoga*.

Silence. When any one of the foregoing aids has been utilised by the subject, sooner or later he must enter into the silence, for it is during silence that he passes from the suggestible state the aids have produced into the true trance state.

Duration. This is a very individual question, depending on the temperament, endurance, and particular needs of the subject. Because of the dangers that can attend trance meditation, it is well, to begin with, to submit to direction from a virtuous and well-instructed adept.

The Return. This should be gentle. Gradually the state wears off. It is possible to control duration with practice; there should be no hurry or sudden break. No other person should try to shake the subject out of trance. The shock could be dangerous.

Replenishment. The subject will generally feel hungry and thirsty after trance. He should have prepared for himself in advance a simple repast. Performing a magic rite often causes the temperature of the subject to rise, but trance states cause it to fall. A warm wrap should be at hand for the return.

Record. It is worthwhile to write down in a notebook details of duration, depth, experiences, and so on for future study and reference.

Sensation. To begin with, breathing may be fast, then deep and laboured. Finally it will seem to cease almost altogether. The focus of attention, if not directed outwards towards a meditation object, is in the centre of the brow – sometimes in the navel or genital centres. The eyes, whether open or closed, tend to come together as though directed at the tip of the nose or they may turn upwards – the pupils disappearing under the eye-lids. The pupils themselves may be either dilated and of a dark hue, rolled back, leaving the white exposed.

The experience is at first of sinking backwards into the self. Then this movement of the psyche can be directed downwards, plane by plane, into the depths of consciousness – the underworld. Or it might be directed upwards plane by plane, as though ascending the Tree of Life. Such movements are called sinking or rising on the planes. Projection to a distance is known as astral travelling.

Possession. In this kind of trance, the subject has the experience that his own psyche has been put to sleep or banished, and that he is possessed or taken over by another human psyche, dead or alive, or by an angel or demon. In a higher state, infilled by a divine entity, a god.

Individual Participation. Here, the subject has the experience of his psyche moving out of his body and joining in activities with the psychic or astral bodies of others. For example, the flight to the witches' sabbat and partaking in rites and revelries there, or entering a fairy ring or hollow hill and joining the fairies in dancing and feasting; at a higher level, being taken up by a god and entering the kingdom of the gods. In the different Tarot initiations – for the Path of Initiation described in the previous chapter is only one of many – the disciple experiences meetings with different personnages of the Tarot, and appearing to undergo actual tests with them.

Group Participation. Here the subject is merged with the group, and loses his identity in it, as occurs in tribal rites and dances. On the other hand, the subject might lose his identity in the kind of mass hysteria typical of a Hitler rally, a negro-lynching, or the less fortunate aspects of university student and police behaviour today.

The nature and technique of trance has been gone into at some length as this detailed knowledge is essential for the dedicated seer who wishes to read, through vision, the records of past ages as well as of the past histories of individuals; that kind of seer who wants to be aware of present trends in world affairs as well as in the problems of those who consult him; he who wishes to pierce the veil hiding the future of mankind as well as of the individual. He wants to be able to enter into a higher or deeper realm of experience at will, recognising dangers and having safeguards. Furthermore, should he wish to communicate with those shades believed to be of the dead and give their comforting messages to the living – that is, if he is a medium as some magi are – he must understand and control the trance state necessary for this kind of operation. And should he wish to work with angelic or demoniacal forces, with fairies – who are not to be considered with the usual sentimentality – or to partake in a witches' coven, he must have a thorough knowledge of trance.

The dangers of trance practice are an ever-present problem. There is the danger of disturbing the balance of the mind, or of those of unbalanced mind being drawn to practise going into trance. There is the danger of hysteria, of being out of control of one's actions while under trance, and of misleading others by communicating a false vision or misreading a vision. There is the danger of communicating terror, anxiety, hate, or envy, and aiding and abetting others in trying to take revenge at a distance. Then there is the danger of being possessed by an unsavoury or vindictive entity or of gaining a neurotic hold over another human being and enslaving him, or of harmfully influencing a whole group of people, even whole nations. Conversely, through the passivity of trance, the practitioner may become enslaved to another or to the powers of the Left Hand Path.

The best and only complete safeguard is a good and noble character, for no evil can touch him who is virtuous, wise, and compassionate. Evil and harm can come only to him who himself is prone to evil and harmfulness, and is without love. The magus of the Right Hand Path must ever work on the perfection of the self.

TRANCE MEDITATION AND THE TAROT CARDS

The seer who wishes to plumb the depths hidden within each of the Tarot cards and to have, at least, the inner experience of initiation following the three times seven steps as indicated in the previous chapter, should daily retire into his sanctum and enter into a light trance state while seated before the cards and selecting one for each day. Mounting by way of the steps of initiation he will work first of all with the greater arcana. Only later will he supplement this by a painstaking study of the fifty-six cards of the lesser arcana. Most examples of the Tarot cards are large, and it is easy, therefore, to fix each card to a board and stand it up on the table so that the card is level with the eyes of the seer and be placed at such a distance that every detail is visible. No matter how many times the seer reviews each card or several cards in conjunction, he will be amazed to discover how many new meanings, greater depths and higher illuminations are disclosed to him.

The Intellectual Approach. The seer will in all probability start in this way, in which a trance state is hardly necessary. He will have read about the cards, compared different methods for using them and the variations in meaning applied to them. He will approach their symbols rationally, that is, he will try to grasp their meanings with the conscious mind. Some cards may seem very clear in their symbolism, royal personages for example, but some may puzzle and intrigue him, such as the Pope Joan card. Some will fit the Christian tradition, the Pope, the Devil, and the Angel of the Judgment. Others may baffle him, the tower struck by lightning or the moon with the cray-fish in the tank below. The hanged man is another obscure symbol. He will begin a study of so-called heretical sects, and also the traditions of the secret societies – Gnostic, Hermetic, Cathar, Rosicrucian, Masonic and so on – seeing where symbols have been drawn from these. Such studies open the way to an investigation into possible earlier sources such as Egyptian, Chaldean, and Greek. Eventually his knowledge concerning the Tarots will be extensive even though little is known as yet about their history. He may, by his researches, be able to add facts or speculations of value in this unusual field.

The Divinatory Approach. At first this may seem to the serious student to be unworthy of consideration as being one of the arts of vulgar magic suitable for gypsy fortune tellers only. But it is doubtful if he can resist for long the temptation to have his cards read even if he is determined not to believe a word. And then he will want to try his hand at reading the cards himself. After a while he will discover that there is more to divination than he thought, and he will begin to study the many different kinds of divination that men have resorted to in the past or in different parts of the world today. The study of divination will inevitably lead to a consideration of trance states.

The Initiatory Approach. Now the seer puts aside his intellectual studies and appreciation of the simpler of the divinatory arts and begins the more advanced method of trance experience.

Seated before one of the Tarots with eyes steadily fixed upon it he quietly enters trance, which need not be of a very deep nature at first. Later, when he has gained confidence in his ability to control himself under trance, he will be able to let himself go more fully.

Such experiences are so individual that one may well hesitate to try to describe one or more of them. However, the attempt must be made. It should always be born in mind that an experience is a living thing, neither the mind of the seer nor the vibrations from the cards can be static. There is a continuous changing in both. In trying to recall an experience and to note it down there is a crystallisation that, while inevitable, is yet false, being static. The actual experience is rather like being at a motion-picture show in which one is both spectator and participator at the same time.

Gazing fixedly at the card it by turn may seem to grow larger or smaller, to approach or to recede. Then it may vanish altogether. A common experience is the feeling that the floor of the room has changed into a large chess board with its black and white squares upon which the Tarot personages stand, move, and play their parts – an *Alice Through the Looking Glass* experience. Another is to see a circle covering most of the floor within which the Tarot personages play their roles. In this case the table either disappears or shrinks to a size that allows it to fit into one of the squares or to take up only a small space in the circle. This is a trance vision in which enlargement – the board, circle and personages – or diminishment – the shrinking of the table – is experienced. Another experience in trance diminishment is to see board or circle and personages in miniature on the table surface. It is then as if the seer had the immensity of a Gulliver in relation to the Lilliputian personages of the Tarot. The movement of the personages is generally of a gliding nature, as though they moved in the stately measures of a minuet, although there are times when frenzy seems to come upon them, and chaos results.

The movements of the fool are often jaunty; those of the lovers, tender, sad, or ecstatic. The hanged man seems to dance or jump, while angels may flutter, demons caper, and hierophants and emperors move in stately fashion. Sun, moon, and stars revolve. The various beasts seem to move rather like puppets. In some states of trance vision plants and flowers can actually be seen growing, unfolding, bearing fruits, and withering. Time and space have different rates and dimensions under trance. A flash of lightning, a falling brick or stone, the blast of a trumpet, these can send shudders through the frame of the seer. The experience of beauty is indescribable, as is that of horror. Similar contrasts have been noted by those who have experimented with mescalin.

Colour. The vision of colour is stimulated by the

actual colours that appear on the cards although printers have not always adhered to the right symbolic use of these, either through ignorance or because of technical difficulties in making the blocks. Red indicates the earth, warmth, blood, the sun, royalty, and earth gods. Blue indicates the heavens, the cold, astral fluids, the moon, angels, and high gods. Yellow indicates material things, power, corn, bounty. Green indicates the land of fairy, nature, elemental forces, perversity. Brown indicates strength, toil, hunting divinities, the witches' coven. There is a tendency for the cups to have an aura of yellow, blue, and some red; swords, blue and red with some yellow; platters, yellow and red with some blue; wands, red and yellow with some blue. But colours are constantly changing according to the particular role the card is playing at any given moment. It could be said that when the outer robe of a personage is blue and the under robe red, there is a heaven aspect predominating as, similarly, when the outer robe is red and the under one blue, the reverse is indicated. A multi-coloured garb suggests the combination of all four elements – earth, air, fire and water.

Speech. It is sometimes asked if the Tarot personages speak or appear to speak to the seer in trance. There is certainly the perception of sound, for fairy music can be heard as well as the reverberations of thunder and the sound of the trumpet. However, the experience is rather that words from the personages are heard inwardly by the seer. But then, all these trance experiences may be completely subjective, although there are magi who claim that there are objective experiences also.

Dimensions, Space, and Time. It has already been mentioned that the seer sometimes seems giant-like in comparison with the tiny personages. There are also times, however, when he is of similar size and seems to be moving with them about the board or circle. Space seems to change according to the needs of the initiation drama being enacted. For example, distant mountains really appear to be far away, the chess board extending itself into space for this purpose. The journey to the mountains and over them is arduous and takes time. However the sense of time does change, for something can happen almost instantaneously that ordinarily would take many hours. The personages and the accessories they use seem to have dimension and weight although a lightness and transparency, not perceptible in the day-to-day world, is noticeable, and everything tends to be surrounded by an aura or to be somehow illuminated from within.

Bodily Sensations. In attempting some crudely materialistic or scientific explanation of the body and brain mechanism of trance, it was said that the senses were temporarily cut off from the hypothalamus which continued somehow to function on its own, and the question arose as to what in that state activated it. If there really is such a break, to what in the human constitution under trance do the sensations of hearing, sight, touch, smell, and taste make themselves perceptible? The occult answer might be that the senses and their responses under trance are those of the astral body and not of the dense physical body, for this interpretation propounds an astral counterpart to every physical manifestation. Indeed the physical body is moulded on an astral pattern, using some kind of condensation of so-called matter for objective material manifestation. The seer in trance feels heat and cold, hears music, tastes food, experiences passion, and so on, but always on planes less dense than the physical, that is, on the astral. So that his appetites and their satisfaction are ethereal, and no matter how much he may have eaten at a fairy banquet he will return to the mundane world hungry. We might think here of the Devil's trick of giving money to a man, who on returning home, takes from his wallet nothing but dry leaves.

Incubi and Succubi. It may be asked if under trance conditions the personages of the Tarot enter into carnal relationships with the seer. If so, they might be approximated to incubi and succubi, but not necessarily evil as those entities are supposed to be. It should be remembered how many phenomena known to occultists have been condemned by the Church, and that descriptions of them, as well as of the teachings and practices of so-called heretics, have mostly been recorded by the hostile pens of ecclesiastics. There is no just reason to suppose that astral lovers, for example, are evil spirits. Quite the contrary. An incubus, so the Church Fathers taught, was one of God's angels who fell through lusting after women. Such an angel they said, was transformed into a lewd demon. In France, a spirit such as this is called *follet*, in Germany *alb*, in Italy *folletto*, and in Spain *duende*. A female spirit of this kind is called a succubus, who is said to seduce men. She often appears as a wood nymph, just as the male often appears as a faun. The spirit of the Tarot card, The Moon, could be an *incubus* or a *succubus* when representing the morbid or nightmare quality of this card. Both *incubi* and *succubi* can change their sex at will or appear as hermaphroditic. *Incubus* has the meaning 'to lie upon' hence both the horse demon of the nightmare and the demon or angel lover who lies upon the sleeper, or upon one in trance. A shaman will say that the spirit body may leave someone in trance and visit another person for good or ill, hence a 'spooky' lover may well be a neighbour and not a spirit creature.

Magical practices such as are carried out with the Tarot in trance are based on a system of polarities or opposites. Yet in the final analysis unity is proclaimed. The cosmic 'all', the unmanifest, is 'one'. Only as it becomes manifest does duality appear. From the unknown reservoir of unformed life, the coagulations of density are extruded. This descent of thickening matter sinking to those tangible experiences known to us of this earth, are necessary for earth conditions in which our souls can objectify themselves and reproduce.

The duality of manifesting powers that we call good and evil, as Zoroaster (628–551 BC) taught, are necessary to maintain the world in which we live. Ahura Mazda, Lord of Light and the Sun of the Tarot appears as opposed to Angra Mainya, the Lord of Darkness, the Devil of the Tarot. They are the positive and negative of the battery of the universe and as the occultist knows are not, ultimately, either good or evil in themselves. The Tarots both reveal this duality and offer a reintegration. When the true teaching has been received what then could be truthfully called black magic and of the Left Hand and what, white magic and of the Right Hand? Who could in fact be rightly styled a black magician or a black witch?

5
The Art and Science of Palmistry

'YOUR fortune in your hand, kind sir. Cross the gypsy's palm with silver. What luck the future holds for you!'

On the hands are written for those who can read their language, that which has gone before, that which is, and that which will surely come to pass.

CHIROMANCY OR DIVINATION FROM THE MARKINGS ON THE HAND

The art of hand reading or palmistry. Its origins are lost in the mists of time. It is known in India as *Hastrika yoga*. It was and is diffused throughout the East. It is a common art-science in every corner of the modern world. It was known to and revered by the Greeks. Anaxagoras (500–428 BC) gave instructions in it to his disciples. Aristotle (384–322 BC) spoke of it. It has been told that he discovered a book of instructions on an altar of Hermes in Egypt, which he passed on to Alexander the Great. The supposed text of this magic and mythical book was later rendered into Latin by

Hispanus. In the 15th century of our era two books on
the art came from the presses that had given the world
our first printed Bibles. These were entitled *Die Kunst
Ciromanta* (1475) and *Cyromantia Aristotelis cum
Figuris* (1490).

Good King Hal of England forbade the study and
practice by law but his progressive daughter, Queen
Bess, reinstated it, valuing it so highly that she created
Dr John Dee her Royal Palmist and Astrologer. Most
famous of recent exponents was that master reader,
Cheiro. Such masters apart, gypsy mothers have certain
additional comments to make when teaching their children the art, a few of which will be added to this
general survey of the theory and practice of this means
of divination.

Divination from the markings on the hand is based
chiefly on the lines of the hand. The seven major lines
are:
1. *The Life Line*. The Vital.
2. *The Head Line*. The Natural.
3. *The Heart Line*. The Mensal.
4. *The Girdle of Venus*. The Passional.
5. *The Health Line*. The Hepatica or Line of the
Liver.
6. *The Line of Apollo or the Sun*. The Artistic. Line of
Genius.
7. *The Line of Saturn*. Fate or Destiny Line.
   The seven minor lines are:
1. *The Line of Mars*. The Line of Strength.
2. *The Via Lascivia*. The Sister Health Line.
3. *The Line of Intuition*.
4. *The Line of Marriage*.

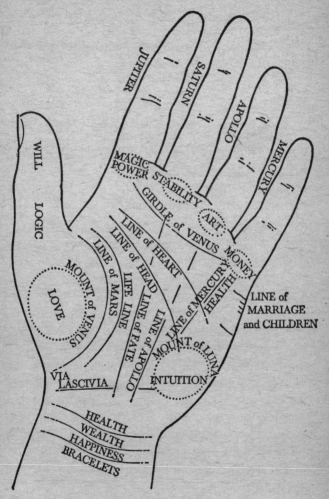

Figure 6.   The Hand

5. *The Line of Well-Being.* ⎫
6. *The Line of Wealth.*   ⎬ The Three Bracelets.
7. *The Line of Happiness.*   ⎭

Lines that show stars, spots, forks, tassels, waves, doubles, chains, islands, crosses or squares may be read as follows:

A Star on a Mount. Fame. In a weak hand, morbidity.

A Spot. Generally an illness.

A Fork. Divided interests. Psychological problems.

A Tassel. Dispersed efforts.

A Wave. Changeability. Travel.

A Doubled Line. Reinforcement.

A Chain. Instability.

An Island. Temporary blockage.

A Cross. A shock.

A Square. Protection.

Upward branches point to success; downward branches the reverse. Breaks are malefic.

The interpretation of such marks is so abstruse an art that it is better not to give more than the foregoing list which only mentions the more obvious of meanings and should in no way be accepted as dogmatic.

The left hand is generally said to concern the natural or inherited character and the imprints of the collective unconscious. The right hand concerns individual efforts at character formation and the impact of society upon the subject.

CHIROGNOMY

This is the aspect of the art dealing with the shapes of the hands and fingers. In principle there are seven different hand formations, but in practice many minglings or variations of these will be encountered.

THE SEVEN GENERAL FORMATIONS

1. *The primitive*. Animal-like, natural, possibly low or bestial.
2. *The square*. Practical, capable, possibly brutal.
3. *The spatulate*. Active, nervous, possibly mentally cruel.
4. *The 'knobbly'*. Philosophical, possibly over-pedantic.
5. *The pointed*. Artistic, refined, possibly over-punctilious.
6. *The slender*. Clairvoyant, aesthetic, possibly morbid.
7. *The integrated*. Multiple or diverse qualities.

THE DIGITS

The three phalanges of the thumb concern:
1. *The Will*. First or top phalange.
2. *Logic*. Second or middle phalange.
3. *Love*. Third phalange at the base.
   The shapes and joints of the fingers indicate:
1. Intuition when square with smooth joints.
2. Sensitivity and impulsiveness when pointed with smooth joints.
3. Rationality and methodicalness when having large joints.

The shape of the fingers themselves indicate:

1. *Large*. Painstaking and slow.
2. *Short*. Impulsive and hasty.
3. *Thick and short*. Selfish or self-centred.
4. *Curved and stiff*. Fearful or cautious.
5. *Backward curving and subtle*. Attractive but inquisitive.
6. *Crooked or deformed*. Irritable or malicious.
7. *Puffy*. Hedonistic.
8. *Well-separated fingers*. Independent, freedom loving.

THE PALMS

1. *Thin and dry*. A nervous disposition.
2. *Thick and soft*. A sensuous nature.
3. *Firm*. An energetic character.
4. *Flabby*. A lazy or phlegmatic tendency.
5. *Hollow and with few mounts*. Prone to ill health.

THE HANDS AND NAILS

Large hands show ability for work and attention to details, while small hands show a breadth of vision with conceptual thinking.

The nails may be long, short, or broad. By studying their shape, texture, and markings, illnesses may be predicted or diagnosed.

THE MOUNTS

1. *Venus* indicating the passions.
2. *Jupiter* indicating the will to power.

3. *Saturn* indicating stability of character.
4. *Apollo* indicating artistic gifts.
5. *Mercury* indicating financial ability and the need to travel.
6. *Luna* or *Diana* indicating imaginative qualities but also instability.

DOCTORS AND PALMISTRY

Those materialists who noisily deny that there can be any truth in the palmist's art may well refrain today, for a number of doctors and scientists are coming to think that the study of the hands and their markings can reveal hidden abnormalities such as potential mongolism, heart defects, and leukemia. The cheiromancer has always known of the diagnostical possibilities in hand reading and his proficiency in diagnosing illnesses and suggesting remedies, while less entertaining, often proves of more value than predicting future successes in matters of love, fortune, and renown. The medical study of the lines and creases or ridges in the hand is known as 'dermatographics'. As long ago as 1684 the English physician, Dr Grew, published his report on the ridges in the skin that form our finger prints. These were classified in 1890 by the English scientist Francis Galton and used for identification by criminologists. But not until recently had the medical profession turned a serious eye upon the diagnostical possibilities concealed in the hand.

Now scientists, after considerable research, say that the patterns on the hands are laid down in about the third month of fetal life; they are completed five months before birth. These patterns consist of lines, arches, whirls, loops, Y-shapes, or *triadii* or three-ribbed formations. The distal and proximal transverse flexion creases – heart and head lines to palmists – are normally separated and distinct, and do not extend completely over the hand. But in forty per cent of mongoloids these are replaced by a single transverse simian crease or line similar to the line on the hand of a monkey. This single line is one of the signs indicating abnormality of the chromosomes. Such a sign may be found in the hands of babies born of women who have taken thalidomide, for example, or who have contracted german measles during early pregnancy. The work of Dr Margaret A. Menser and S. G. Purvis-Smith at the Royal Alexandra Hospital for Children, Sydney, Australia, on the relation between such signs indicating subsequent leukemia, is likely to prove of paramount importance in diagnosis, preventive measures, and eventual remedies. The extension of the 'Sydney' line, the head line, or the appearance of the simian line characterised thirty-six per cent of leukemic children as opposed to thirteen per cent of children under investigation. In the medical context one should also mention the astonishing psychological work of Dr Charlotte Wolff on hands and gestures which, she insists, is in no way connected with our chiromantic art, but is diagnostic and therapeutic. Every serious student of the occult would do well to make himself familiar with her theory and practice. Confirmation of much that the seer and the gypsy have handed on to us grows apace. It is possible that the examination of hands may become everyday routine in medical check-ups.

SOME ADVICE ON HOW TO READ HANDS

The palmist seats the subject at his side before a small table in such a way that a strong light either from the window or from a table lamp, falls directly upon the hands under examination. Some readers prefer to have the subject opposite them, but viewing the hands in this way is not all together satisfactory.

A palmist's kit, consisting of an ink roller and finger-print ink with which to take impressions of the hands, is invaluable. After the client has left the palmist can study at leisure the prints taken during consultation and after making a memorandum of his findings, post it to the client, while keeping a copy so that both may be able to refer to it in the future if necessary.

At the beginning of the consultation the palmist will have noted the kind of handshake the client has, and felt the moisture or dryness of his hand. A quick glance will reveal the general shape of the hands and whether the fingers are in harmony with the palms and the whole hand with the overall physique of the client. Scrutinising the left hand and then the right will show what are inherited characteristics and what modifications or developments have occurred since birth. The hands should be held firmly so that the flow of blood makes each line stronger in colour and therefore more easy to read. By turning the hands this way and that, the backs, fronts, textures, undulations, and any deformities may be ascertained. Then the shapes of the fingers and the type of nails must have attention. A detailed description of the lines, mounts and markings such as stars, squares or doubles may now be given. It is usual to start with the life line, but each reader has his preferences or may change his mode of procedure according to the subject under consideration.

A WARNING

Never predict the year of death, but rather promise a long life and a fulfilled life. Take great care not to alarm the client by talking of serious illnesses or accidents to come. This is not to say that one must be dishonest in a reading but careful investigation will show how dangers in the future may be avoided or surmounted. Destiny is written in the hands, but Divinity has the power to change that which seems bound to come to pass. Miracles do happen and the palmist can work with God by imparting to the subject the faith necessary for their coming about. The efficacy of positive suggestion, sympathy, and helpful advice is known to the magus as well as to the psychologist and the physician. The palmist must feel humble both before the writing of fate upon the hands and the power of ever-creative life to use that which has been written to the best advantage. If the subject has a copy of the prints of his hands and a written account given to him by the palmist, then at other sessions character traits can be agreed to or disputed and each event predicted – either as it comes to pass or does not – may be ticked off. Having such a plan of coming events the subject will be able to prepare himself in such a way that he may take full advantage of the beneficent or take steps to surmount the malefic. Sometimes the gift of clairvoyance is so strong that a palmist cannot help, but if he is forced to do this he must at once seek a remedy for the ill-fortune decreed. At the end of a consultation a clearly-worded summing-up of all that has been read in the hands is of great help to those who take the art and science of palmistry seriously.

When called upon to read a number of hands in succession, at a charity fair for example, the palmist cannot hope to plunge deeply into an investigation of each client who pays his five shillings in a good cause. Like the gypsy giving a quick reading as she tags along beside one in the street, the reader must have an easy patter and a number of cheerful predictions suitable for all and sundry. Such a reading should be taken for what it is, an amusing indulgence that may raise funds in some worthwhile cause. All the same there are moments when the truth will out and a startling prediction may break through a routine reading.

AN EXAMPLE OF A QUICK READING
GIVEN IN THE GYPSY'S CARAVAN

'Madame, from the backs of your hands I see that you are of a happy disposition. From the palms that you are warm-hearted. The fluting of your nails show lung trouble in youth but you are quite healed now. Your fingers show quickness and intuition. Jupiter shows thoughtfulness. However your instinctual nature is at war with your respectable environment. Your mounts show Venus and Luna dominating – ah, what passion, what imagination, madame! Excuse me for saying so, but your heart line shows a flirtatious trend. I fear that you may be very fickle where love is concerned, but in friendship you are more steady. A strong, clearly-marked life line; illness is behind you, many years of health lie ahead. You manage your own business I think. Why? Because your excellent head line and the finger of Mercury tell me so. Look at those bracelets of health, wealth and happiness. I envy you those, indeed I do! Thumb strong, a little domineering. First finger, yes, practicality. Finger of Saturn, a little weak; no good for gambling, certainly not. Apollo tells me that you are married to an artist. Ah well, so *you* have to earn the living. Three lovely children; a boy and two girls I should say. That little affair of the heart on the side, perhaps we had better not go into that? You really want to know? Fun while it lasts but it won't last long. Yes, they do say . . . a little of what you fancy does you good! All the same, prudence, madame, prudence. Of course, if you like to donate another five shillings to our good cause, madame, this gypsy will be delighted to tell you more!'

6

Numerology and Divination by the Casting of Lots

NUMEROLOGY

THE art of divining through numbers must be as old as the ability to count and to make recordings with shells, pebbles, by knotting string, and by drawing signs and pictures. And with these signs of numbers and letters went words, grunted or chanted. No doubt it was the medicine man or seer of the tribe who invented this great magic. So men became free of dependency on memory and able to communicate by means of the written word and number. Such a tremendous invention the seer-priest attributed to a god, and therefore letters, numbers, words, and sentences held a numenous as well as a utilitarian character. A number was not used solely to count with, nor was a letter or combination of letters, a symbol-indication of a thought, message, or recording of a mundane nature; but both had the additional value of magical properties and powers. Numbers and letters could be used to conjure forth the aid of the spirits. The spirits bound by the power of these signs could be made to reveal that which was hidden – for divination. From its high place as a means of binding and revealing, of Cabalistic evocation and invocation, number-letter magic has declined, and has been popularised by the fortune-teller as an impressive, if easy, way of ascertaining a person's lucky number, lucky day, with a hint at character reading.

The transmission of this once high, and now for the most part debased, pseudo-science now appears among us as *numerology*. But while we may smile at this stock ingredient of the homely fortune teller's trade – it has even declined to the level of the fun-fair slot machine – we should remember that it is the superficial aspect of a large part of the theory and practice of mystical occultism. Many occultists will tell you that while linguists have translated Egyptian hieroglyphics exoterically, the secret meaning of these remains concealed from the profane. And the same is said of other ancient writings, including even the Hebrew Bible.

The occult theory is that every number and letter has a unique power and that combinations of these powers produce or reveal certain divinatory or magical results; that there is an occult relationship existing between numbers and letters and the whole fabric and machinery of the cosmos. The Greeks were so captivated by the operations of numbers, letters, and the sounds that went with these, that they believed the whole of manifest life to be governed by them. Pythagorus (500 BC) taught that the world is built upon the power of numbers. He maintained that the numerals from 1 to 9 were the universal primaries. Centuries later Cornelius Agrippa (AD 1533), probably borrowing from a secret tradition, listed their significance in his treatise on occult philosophy.

The following list, displayed in many a gypsy prophetess's tent, is derived from his descriptions.

SIGNIFICANCE OF LUCKY NUMBERS 1 TO 9

1. The number of aim, aggression, ambition and action. (Note the association with A, the first letter of the alphabet.) The figure one is the flight of the arrow towards its target of fame! Pause and think – 'the first shall be last and the last shall be first'. This is the number of tyrants. Its sign is the point.

2. The number of balance as well as contrast. Antithesis, opposites, polarities. Of equilibrium and harmony. Of male and female. Its sign is parallel lines.

3. The number of time and fate – past, present, and future. Of the family – father, mother, and child. Of variability and change, but also of adaptability. It signifies a happy and gifted character. Its sign is the triangle.

4. The number of foundation. It represents the points of the compass, the seasons, the elements of earth, air, fire, and water. Called the most primitive among numbers. Its sign is the square.

5. The number of chance. This is both the most propitious and the most hazardous of numbers. Although lacking in stability it links the opposites. Beneficent for adventurers, for new experiences, for those with nimble fingers. Its sign is the keystone of the arch.

6. The number of perfection, being divisible by 2 and by 3. It suggests trust, harmony and beauty. Its sign is the six colours of the rainbow.

7. The magic number. It governs occult mysteries, clairvoyance, and magical operations. It represents the seven principles in man and the universe, the seven planets, days of the week, and the notes of the musical scale. Its sign is the seven-pointed star.

8. The number of earthly triumph. It represents the solid and complete. When halved its parts are equal, thus it holds a fourfold balance. Its sign is the double square.

9. Greatest of all primary numbers. It suggests both hope and achievement. It contains the qualities of all the others. It is composed of three times the number 3, held to be most propitious. By its power the magician controls the forces of nature. Its sign is the sceptre and orb.

Any series of large numbers may be reduced to these primaries. A convenient method is to proceed as follows:

Suppose the number to be reduced is 123. Add each separate figure, that is $1 + 2 + 3 = 6$. Refer to the description of number 6 as outlined above and the divinatory meaning will be found. Or, to take a more complicated example: 57321 or $5 + 7 + 3 + 2 + 1 = 18$ or $1 + 8 = 9$. The number 9 is thus the occult primary of 57321.

TABLE OF DESTINY NUMBERS

Gypsies often carry a set of cards with numbers inscribed on them which are packed in a small open box. Perched on their shoulders are two love-birds.

For a small coin the gypsy will take one of these birds on her finger and let it peck out a card from the box and this is said to represent your lucky number for the day. Beneath the number a short character reading, message, or answer to a wish is printed.

These number messages are somewhat along the following lines:

1. Your lucky day is Sunday. Your lucky number – One. A day for action, ambition and attainment. Face urgent problems on this day, give the rest of time to play. Documents you must not sign, give the day to cakes, love and wine. Your planet is the Sun.

2. Your lucky day is Monday. Your lucky number – Two. A day to plan, to plot and scheme, but no action take. Morning laughter. Evening tears. Kiss before too late. Don't take 'no' for an answer. Don't worry. After midnight luck changes for the better. Your planet is the Moon.

3. Your lucky day is Tuesday. Your lucky number – Three. Sign for money or for love. Make your choices as you will. Lovers' quarrels soon will heal. You are talented, versatile and a fighter, but also love pleasure. Your planet is Mars.

4. Your lucky day is Wednesday. Your lucky number – Four. Work, play, a few tears. No risks give long years. Hard tasks to finish. A journey suggested. Make plans carefully. Be trustworthy, honesty pays. Say 'yes' to one who loves you. Your planet is Mercury.

5. Your lucky day is Thursday. Your lucky number – Five. Lucky for the many, unlucky for the few. Give away money, your love comes to you. Be enthusiastic.

Enjoy the unexpected. You are sure to **win**. Your planet is Jupiter.

6. Your lucky day is Friday. Your lucky number – Six. Not unlucky as some declare, but not a day for games of chance. Of jealousy you must beware, passion breaks a soldier's lance. Success for those with new ideas. A day for friendship and leisure is suggested. Courtship leads to marriage. Your planet is Venus.

7. Your lucky day is Saturday. Your lucky number – Seven. For hints and hunches, pricks and punches. Make the best of it! Study, art, meditation and rest are indicated. Do not let introspection lead to morbidity. Trust the one you love. Your planet is Saturn.

A variety of different predictions, rhyming or hortatory, will be found in the chapbooks sold by the gypsy, a collection of which it is fascinating to make. It will be noted that sometimes the first day of the week is given to Sunday and sometimes the seventh.

THE FIGURE ALPHABET

Every letter has its number. Here is the key:

A	B	C	D	E	F	G	H	I
J	K	L	M	N	O	P	Q	R
S	T	U	V	W	X	Y	Z	
1	2	3	4	5	6	7	8	9

HOW TO FIND YOUR LUCKY BIRTH NUMBER

Take the number of the day, month and year of birth and reduce to the prime number thus:

Date of birth, 31 May 1908. This gives $3 + 1 + 5 + 1 + 9 + 0 + 8 = 27$ or $2 + 7 = 9$. So 9 is the lucky number.

Consult the description of the prime numbers together with the gypsy Table of Destiny, use some clairvoyance and see what you can learn about yourself.

HOW TO FIND YOUR NAME NUMBER

Write down your first name and family name and reduce the letters to numbers using the figure alphabet above. Thus:

Charlotte Dobby gives 38193622546227, totalling 60 for the prime number 6 + 0 = 6. Six is the prime number. Consult the description of the prime numbers and Table of Destiny and see what is to be learnt about this young lady.

NUMBERS IN DAY-TO-DAY LIFE

To discover if any particular day in such and such a person's life was or will be, propitious, proceed by taking the person's birth and name numbers and add these to the date of the day about which information is required. The first example concerns a business transaction which is to take place next Wednesday, the fourth day of the week during May, the fifth month of the year, during 1971. Using the figure alphabet as instructed it will be found that the prime number is 9. Read the indications concerning this number; it will be found that it is most propitious in every way.

In our second example, imagine that we have come upon some old family record concerning a Mr John Jones who was born on 6 May 1870, and wished to go to sea on 1 January 1890. Was this a propitious day for him? Proceed to establish his name number which will be found to be 38, his birth number which is 27, and the date of sailing which works out as 20. The addition of all these numbers and their reduction to the primary gives 4. The indication is that the day was calm (balanced) but storms might be expected (antithesis) but the sign of two parallel lines looks sufficiently calm. It is to be hoped that John Jones kept his sea legs and returned home after his voyage safely!

Such simple number methods should be regarded as a game rather than serious divination, although with a measure of clairvoyance, striking results can sometimes be achieved.

GEMATRIA

The Cabalistic number-word science of Gematria, contrary to the superficialities of the foregoing, is a profound magico-philosophical art that operates with the Hebrew alphabet and the numbers that are identified with its twenty-two letters. This method was eventually extended to the Greek and Latin alphabets.

Cabala was, and is, the theosophy or God-Wisdom of the Jews and Chaldeans. The word means 'to receive' or 'to take over'. It was an oral tradition from time immemorial. Many, but not all, of its doctrines and methods were committed to writing in the middle ages. Such a deep impression did it make upon the seeker after truth that there came to be a Platonic, Neo-Platonic (gnostic), Muslim and Christian Cabala. By means of Cabalistic techniques the secret meanings concealed in the Bible may be unveiled by the wise. The numerological aspect is known as the 'law of correspondences'. This occult law rules that a pattern of corresponding though often apparently different 'things' composes the woof and weft of the cosmos and all therein. Hence numbers and letters correspond, but they also correspond with sound, and more strangely, colour. Some magi have taught that even supernatural beings may be given the appearance of form if the right numerological magic rites are carried out.

Only a hint at the esoteric principles upon which serious numerology is based is possible here. Occultists of both East and West attach high value to this law. They hold that the spiritual affinities of any given object can be deduced so that the spiritual concealed in the mundane can be apprehended. Therefore when those potencies they believe to inhabit inner or higher planes or spheres are to be invoked, they utilise secret methods that fall under the heading of this law – correspondence, affinity, analogy. Cabalists maintain that there are thirty-two concealed planes composed of the Ten Sephirah and the twenty-two Paths linking these, as on the Tree of Life where pattern was used for laying the Tarots. It will be remembered that the greater arcana corresponds to the Hebrew number-letter alphabet. To the profane these are thought of as a series of heavens and hells while for the psychologist they are the different levels of consciousness within the mind.

Perhaps by listening in to the Cabalistic discussions of the magi the humble fortune-teller was able to concoct his simple numerological method of divination and exploit it for a few copper coins at the village fair.

ASTRAGLOMANCY, DIVINATION BY
CASTING LOTS

This ancient method is obviously connected with numerology. Among various methods that of casting numbered dice is the most common. The procedure is to think of any question that falls under one of these headings below, shake, and throw two dice. Add the numbers revealed and consult the list of answers.

Questions

1. Success?
2. Love?
3. Loss?
4. Danger?
5. Desire?
6. Wish?
7. Money?
8. Friends?
9. Travel?
10. Marriage?
11. Children?
12. Home?

Answers

1. Yes
2. No
3. Take care
4. Be wise
5. What luck
6. Of course
7. Have faith
8. Patience
9. Certainly
10. Doubtful
11. Nonsense
12. A chance

As a parlour game it is amusing for a few friends to compose lists of questions and answers for themselves

7

Conclusion: Crystal Gazing and the Spirits of the Dead

DEEP in a crystal ball, beneath the troubled surface of a bowl of water, from the movements of the ouija-board, the knocks of the tipping table, the darting of the automatic writer, or the mouthings of one in trance – strange events show themselves. Do the spirits speak?

Yes, assure and demonstrate the seers and witches, and who can prove or disprove their claims?

Somewhat entranced oneself, one assists at these experiences. Afterwards the rational self seeks to explain.

CRYSTAL GAZING

Who cannot visualise a picture of the gypsy woman gazing into her crystal ball on its velvet covered stand before her on the table; her anxious client seated opposite? The darkness of the caravan is only dispelled a little by the light of a candle flickering close to her left hand. A whiff of smouldering herbs assails the nostrils. Perhaps one might be the client, or indeed the prophetess herself!

For scrying with the crystal the gift of clairvoyance is essential, together with a lengthy training by a master of the art. All that can be said concerning the technique is that the ability to go into trance at will – a trance deep enough for visions to appear and yet not so deep that power to describe these is lost, accompanied by an intuitive knowledge of what such visions portend – must be augmented by some kind of occult initiation.

Two kinds of vision may appear in the crystal: they may be either small, highly realistic, moving pictures in glorious technicolour showing events in the past or future, or at a distance, or they may be symbolic images, abstract or figurative. To interpret the latter the interpreter should have a profound knowledge of the meaning of symbols, but this can be acquired. A royal road to such knowledge leads through constant meditation before the Tarots.

To list but a few symbols that are not always in evidence among the cards:

a *Crown* – glory, responsibility;

a *Skull* – death, but also wisdom;

a *Mask* – deceit, tragedy;

a *Star* – success, but also a warning;

a *Globe* – travel;

a *Serpent* – health, knowledge, but also temptation;

Scales – justice, but also equilibrium or the reverse;

a *Lighthouse* – hope, but also storms and danger;

Crossed Swords – a quarrel;

an *Eye* – forethought, good luck, but can be evil;

a *Beetle* – long life;

a *Water Lily* – creativity;

a *Frog* – fertility, also concealed blessings;

a *Bird* – a message, also immortality, rebirth;

a *Fruit* – children;

an Anchor – safety, hope;
a Heart and Dagger – great suffering.

THE PLANCHETTE OR OUIJA-BOARD, THE INVERTED WINE GLASS, THE TABLE, AND THE AUTOMATIC WRITER

For planchette or ouija-board divination a light wood (or plastic) triangle mounted on tiny runners and having a pencil at its apex is placed on a large sheet of paper. Two people lay their hands lightly on this board and pass into a semi-trance. Soon the board will move about the paper, uninfluenced – consciously at any rate – by the hands upon it. It will begin to inscribe words, messages, or symbolic drawings. When it 'tires' these may be interpreted. Another method is to write the alphabet in a circle on the paper. Write 'yes' to the right and 'no' to the left and make a line of numbers from one to ten within the circle. Toyshops sometimes sell these triangles and lettered boards for a modest price. The triangle will then be able to answer questions put to it by a simple 'yes' or 'no'. Or it can spell out its messages by running to the different letters that will form these. A similar procedure is followed when using the inverted wine glass on which the index fingers of the participants' hands are placed. The surface must be very smooth to allow the glass to travel over it with ease. In table tipping a code is established with say, one tap for 'yes', two taps for 'no', and an ascending numerical tapping for the alphabet. Several people may sit at the table with both hands on it, each with thumb tips touching and the little finger touching lightly that of his neighbour. All being well, after a few minutes the table will begin to move, rise, and tap out its messages. It may even leave the floor completely or cause the sitters to rise and follow it about the room. The automatic writer method needs but a pencil and several pages of paper. The sitter holds the pencil poised above the paper until it seems to insist on making marks and eventually writing messages. It can be induced to answer questions. The trance state must not be too deep or the sitter tends to fall asleep. For these methods it is both a help and a safeguard to have someone as a witness in the room. Such a person will be able to detect frauds and can also note down messages given by the ouija, the wine glass, or the table. These notes can be filed for future reference or for translation, because sometimes the messages are given in a foreign tongue or in antique phrases long out of use. For example, a frequent communicator through these methods revealed that he was a buccaneer who had sailed the Spanish main. He 'spoke' the Spanish of many years ago in a 'foreign' way. He was not actually a Spaniard it transpired, but had come from elsewhere, picking up Spanish as being the most usual and useful language in the Caribbean. And there was a jolly 13th-century monk who, according to these ouija messages, spoke an uncouth French because, although he had lived in a monastery near Paris, had in fact, or so it seemed, come originally from Schleswig-Holstein. Having recorded these messages it was necessary to obtain the help in interpreting them from linguistic scholars. It should be noted that there is no need to be solemn when practiseing these arts. Often laughter and a happy atmosphere is an aid. And the 'spirits' themselves will sometimes play tricks and make all kinds of unlikely claims or talk utter nonsense, and may later give a message of apology for their unseemly behaviour!

MEDIUMISM

There are those who have the gift for going into deep trance and allowing what are assumed to be the spirits of the dead – as well as disembodied entities such as spirit guides, astral masters or divine and semi-divine beings – to use them as a medium or vehicle through which to speak to us earthly creatures. Some mediums seem even to have the power to make such entities materialise. This technique is fraught with danger, both from fraud and from hysteria. It is best carried out under kind, protective, test conditions. The medium is seated in a chair, lightly clad; and in a warm room with subdued lighting. The light from a red lantern or shaded table lamp is considered most suitable. Breathing deeply, the medium passes into a trance. The watchers will notice after a while that a change comes over the appearance, breathing, and posture of the medium. Then a voice, quite unlike his or her normal one, delivers various messages. Questions may be asked and responses gained. As such a method is extremely fatiguing the medium should not be pushed to continue for too long. A period of silence will allow a return to normality. Again, careful note-taking should accompany this type of clairvoyant expression.

CONCLUDING REMARKS

Can we now draw the threads of homely fortune-telling wisdom together and attempt to find the sources from which these methods of divination spring?

Between the abracadabra of the fortune teller and the inspired words of the prophet there exists a link. That link is to be sought in the secret doctrines of the wise, in the perennial wisdom of occult transmission. Some of this knowledge may be gained from the written word, but if initiation is obtained at the hands of a master, then through oral transmission and sheer physical proximity far more than mere words can be revealed. Dangers there are, but is there anything worthwhile that is not accompanied by an element of risk?

In this book on fortune telling in which cards, hands, crystals, numbers, and trance mediumistic methods – practised by the humble as well as the exalted throughout the world – have been outlined, the stress has not been upon mere superstition but upon the hope that, by repeated practice and careful note-taking of successes and failures, a more scientific investigation of the validity of these methods may be initiated. Such an investigation has already been carried out by Rhine, with ESP.

COSMOLOGICAL VIBRATIONS REPRESENTED BY AN ALGEBRA OF SYMBOLS AND NUMBERS

Objects such as Tarots, lines on the hand, trance-scenes, dice-pips and even tea leaf patterns, grains of sand, or the fall of sticks, do not have symbols and numerological values assigned to them in an arbitrary fashion, but in accordance with the deepest principles of esoteric cosmology far too abstruse to discuss here. An indication as to their nature is all that space will allow. The teaching is somewhat as follows.

Manifesting life, what we know as existence, came and comes into various degrees of materialisation during different phases of what is known as the 'logoidal cycle'. The 'forms' of these phases are built of occult 'atoms' or units arranging themselves in ever greater complexities, their outstanding character being their inevitable trend towards organisation. They are force in cyclic motion, infinitely minute vortices. They are not all of a kind. Among them are varying movement patterns. Some trace an angular path while others follow a three-, four-, five-, six-, or seven-sided orbit.

The gradual condensation of such vibrations bring into being a series of planes of existence ranging from etherical heights to the depths of materialisation. Each of these many planes is extruded from the logoidal primal source and each has its own type of occult atoms with their own kind of movement or vibration. These form the typical 'life pattern' or consciousness of each plane. The occultist speaks of consciousness as being the stuff of a plane, for he holds that *mind not matter is the fabric of life and seeming form.*

Each plane is said to have a planet as its focal point. To put it another way, when each seminal life-wave is ejected from the source, it builds its own consciousness adapted to its function, goal, or type of organisation, and its particular planet is the result of this creative effort.

Thus is postulated a relationship or correspondence between a certain type of atom, a special planet, and a unique state of consciousness. The fundamental or prime atom of any plane has a number of tangents in its orbit which will determine its vibratory rhythm or movement pressing towards its own goal through its drive to organisation. The complexities of any particular plane will be built of its special type of atoms and has a basic number of these with which to organise. The vibratory rhythms of these planes are the fabric of manifestation from the least to the most dense, and can be expressed in mathematical terms. The significance of number for the occultist is thus obvious.

The primary numbers are considered sacred or numenous holding as they do the magic formulae of the – to us – invisible forces which are the mainspring of existence; the pattern behind all things visible and invisible. A knowledge of this cosmic law enables a prophet like Nostradamus to predict the moment of important events to come. Initiates can learn of the birth and death of nations, the coming of a messiah, the hour when men of our earth will take off for another planetary home, with extraordinary exactitude.

The number of planes, spheres, or principles of consciousness have been charted in different ways by different schools of the occult and have been reduced for convenience to ten or thirty-two by Cabalists and seven by the Theosophists, but it is to be clearly understood that there are a vast number of sub-planes grouped under these simplified schemes and that, as the whole cosmos is a living existence or consciousness, there is a constant interpenetration of one plane by another.

The occult investigator has his own methodology but as this is designed to explore and establish that which seems beyond the sensory or normal, proof that would meet the requirements of science is not available. His discoveries remain in the remoter fields of psychology. However the gap between the normal and the supranormal has lessened of late, and a place for parapsychology, extra-sensory experience, and a new attitude to time and space as well as biological investigation and mathematics, is all but permitted.

If ESP is proven, not alone in telepathy but in those other supranormal realms, superstition will give place to an awesome certainty concerning foreseeing and backward-looking. The question, 'what is mind', will call for an ever-extending answer. This quest for a greater widening of horizons, if successful, will lead to truths that are bound to be epoch-making.

Gypsies and witches like the magi can only tell us that they are constantly on the lookout for signs and portents. When some special knowledge is required they scrutinise certain things to which they give a magical value – cards, hands, crystals. Or they make use of movable objects of a numenous character – ouija-boards, wine glasses, tables. Or again, they invite living creatures to work for them, the choice made by love-birds, a message by a flight of swallows, the behaviour 'talk' of a cat. To those who watch and wait in trance, the spirits speak. Thus the unknown becomes known.

When in such a state of expectancy, premonitions fill the mind, emotions shake the body, a deeper consciousness is aroused; one is *en rapport* with a greater consciousness, that of the whole of nature – even greater – that of the Cosmic All. An act of pure attention is needed. Then intuition takes over and prophetic words fall from the quivering lips of the possessed who is under the spell of that for which there is no name.

Then the gods speak.

Further Reading

H. P. Blavatsky, *The Secret Doctrine*, Theosophical Publishing Co, 1888

Richard Cavendish (ed.), *Man, Myth & Magic, An Encyclopedia*, Purnell, 1970

Cheiro, *Language of the Hand*, Corgi, 1968

Aleister Crowley, 777, revised edition

G. de Purucker, *Occult Glossary*, Theosophical Books, 1957

Dion Fortune, *Training and Work of an Initiate*, Aquarian Press

John Fowles, *The Magus*, Jonathan Cape, 1966

William James, *Varieties of Religious Experience*, Collins, 1960

D. H. Lawrence, *Mornings in Mexico and Etruscan Places*, Heinemann, 1956

Eliphas Lévi, *Key of Mysteries*, Rider, 1959

S. L. Macgregor Mathers, *The Kabbalah Unveiled*, Routledge & Kegan Paul, 1957

B. I. Rakoczi, *The Painted Caravan*, L. J. C. Boucher, Holland, 1954

G. G. Scholem, *Major Trends in Jewish Mysticism*, Thames & Hudson, 1955

Henri Sérouya, *La Kabbale*, Editions Grasset, Paris, 1947

Charles Williams, *The Greater Trumps*, Faber & Faber, 1954

Oswald Wirth, *Le Tarot des Imagiers du Moyen Age*, Editeur du Symbolisme, Paris, 1927

ABOUT THE AUTHOR

Basil Ivan Rakoczi is a poet and artist who has writter extensively on occultism and gypsy lore, and is the author of a book on the gypsy Tarot, *The Painted Caravan*. Now living in Paris, and a Quaker, he was born in England and brought up as a Roman Catholic. His Hungarian father and his Irish mother were both students of gypsy beliefs.

ACKNOWLEDGMENTS

The author wishes to express his gratitude to Mrs Escha Wiren for reading his manuscript and correcting hi English; to Mr and Mrs Eric de Mare, Mrs Diana Owen and Mr Victor Meally for verifying and supplying a num ber of facts and traditions; to Mrs Jacqueline Adam for making a clear typescript of the impulsive writings of thi humble student of the occult. The bibliography speaks fo: the many written sources of knowledge to which he ha had recourse, while his greatest thanks go to those un named and unknown gypsy and near-gypsy masters, seers prophetesses, and witches who have throughout his life imparted the secrets of the arts of fortune telling to him and to whom this book is dedicated.

BASIL IVAN RAKOCZI
Fornalutx, Mallorca, 197(

We are grateful to the following for the illustrations, and for permission to use copyright prints and photographs:
Oxford Illustrators Ltd; Barnaby's Picture Library, 5c Camera Press London, 4; Eve Arnold – Magnum, 9 Mansell Collection, 1, 2, 8, 10; Popperfoto, 7; Radic Times Hulton Picture Library, 5a, 6; William Sargant 5b; John Webb, 3.